Cambridge First Certificate in English 4
with answers

Cambridge First Certificate in English 4

WITH ANSWERS

Examination papers from the University of Cambridge Local Examinations Syndicate

CAMBRIDGE
UNIVERSITY PRESS

PUBLISHED BY THE PRESS SYNDICATE OF THE UNIVERSITY OF CAMBRIDGE
The Pitt Building, Trumpington Street, Cambridge, United Kingdom

CAMBRIDGE UNIVERSITY PRESS
The Edinburgh Building, Cambridge CB2 2RU, UK
40 West 20th Street, New York, NY 10011–4211, USA
477 Williamstown Road, Port Melbourne, VIC 3207, Australia
Ruiz de Alarcón 13, 28014 Madrid, Spain
Dock House, The Waterfront, Cape Town 8001, South Africa

http://www.cambridge.org

First published 2001
Fourth printing 2004

Printed in the United Kingdom at the University Press, Cambridge

ISBN 0 521 64640 5 Student's Book
ISBN 0 521 79770 5 Student's Book with answers
ISBN 0 521 64639 1 Teacher's Book
ISBN 0 521 64638 3 Set of 2 Cassettes

Contents

Thanks and acknowledgements

UCLES would like to thank Vanessa Jakeman and Judith Greet for editing the Student's Book and Teacher's Book.

The publishers are grateful to the following for permission to reproduce copyright material. Whilst every effort has been made to locate the owners of copyright, in some cases this has been unsuccessful. The publishers apologise for any infringement or failure to acknowledge the original sources and will be glad to include any necessary correction in subsequent printings.
Alex McWhirter for the text on p. 5, © *Business Traveller*; *The Times* for the text on p. 6 by Beryl Dixon, © Times Newspapers Limited 1994 and the text on p. 83 by Simon Reeve and Christopher Lloyd, © Times Newspapers Limited 1994; The *Guardian* for the text on pp. 8–9 by Martin Bright, © The *Guardian*; The National Magazine Company for the text on pp. 11–12 by Emma Marsden adapted from *She* October 1992 Supplement, © National Magazine Company; *Model World* (Lodmore Country Park, Weymouth) for the text on p. 31; *The Big Issue* for the text on pp. 34–35 by Mark Simmonds; *Girl About Town* for the text on pp. 37–38 by Kitty Doherty; The *Independent* for the text on p. 58 by Keith Elliott; Paul Foster for the text on pp. 60–61; *Woman's Own* for the text on pp. 63–64 by Abby Edwards; *BBC Music Magazine* for the text on p. 84, reprinted with kind permission of *BBC Music Magazine* (www.bbcmusicmagazine.com); *Nine to Five* for the text on pp. 86–87; W.H. Smith for the text on pp. 89–90; Orion Publishing Group for the text on p. 95; Usborne Publishing for the text on p. 97 adapted from *Usborne New Technology: Information Revolution* by permission of Usborne Publishing, Usborne House, 83–85 Saffron Hill, London, EC1N 8RT.

Text permissions by Jean Kennedy and Sophie Dukan

Photographs (black and white): The Telegraph Colour Library/V.C.L. for p. 60

Drawings: Bryan Reading for p. 32

Colour section
Photographs: Gettyone Stone/Donovan Reese for photograph 1A on p. C1 and photograph 2A on p. C2; The Stock Market Photo Agency for photograph 1B on p. C1, photograph 3C on p. C9 and photograph 4C on p. C10; Ace Photo Agency/Mauritius for photograph 2B on p. C2; Impact Photos for photograph 1C on p. C3, Christophe Bluntzer/Impact, and for photograph 3B on p. C7; Robert Harding Picture Library for photograph 1D on p. C3, RHPL/Liaison International, and for photograph 4B on p. C8; Pictor International for photograph 2C on p. C4, photograph 4A on p. C8, photograph 3D on p. C9 and photograph 4D on p. C10; Eye Ubiquitous/Sean Aidan for photograph 3A on p. C7. Our special thanks to The Bell Language School, Cambridge for permission to use photograph 2D on p. C4.

Artwork: UCLES/Gecko Ltd. for 1E on p. C5 and 2E on p. C6; UCLES/Laura Munton/Gecko Ltd. for 3E on p. C11; Hallmark Cards and The Really Good Card Company for 4E on p. C12.

Picture research by Sandie Huskinson-Rolfe of PHOTOSEEKERS

Design concept by Peter Ducker

Cover design by Dunne & Scully

The cassettes which accompany this book were recorded at Studio AVP, London.

To the student

This book is for candidates preparing for the University of Cambridge Local Examinations Syndicate (UCLES) First Certificate in English Examination (FCE). The FCE examination is widely recognised in commerce and industry and in individual university faculties and other educational institutions.

   The collection of four complete practice tests comprises past papers from the Cambridge First Certificate in English examination set in 1996 and 1997; you can practise these tests on your own or with the help of your teacher.

   The FCE examination is part of a group of examinations developed by UCLES called the Cambridge Main Suite. The Main Suite consists of five examinations that have similar characteristics but are designed for different levels of English language ability. Within the five levels, FCE is at Cambridge Level 3.

Cambridge Level 5 Certificate of Proficiency in English (CPE)
Cambridge Level 4 Certificate of Advanced English (CAE)
Cambridge Level 3 First Certificate in English (FCE)
Cambridge Level 2 Preliminary English Test (PET)
Cambridge Level 1 Key English Test (KET)

The FCE examination consists of five papers:

Paper 1	Reading	1 hour 15 minutes
Paper 2	Writing	1 hour 30 minutes
Paper 3	Use of English	1 hour 15 minutes
Paper 4	Listening	40 minutes (approximately)
Paper 5	Speaking	14 minutes (approximately)

Paper 1   Reading
This paper consists of **four parts**. Each part contains a text and some questions. Part 4 may contain two or more shorter related texts. There are **35 questions** in total, including multiple choice, gapped text and matching questions.

Paper 2   Writing

This paper consists of **two parts**. For both parts you have to write between 120 and 180 words. Part 1 is **compulsory**. It provides texts which are sometimes accompanied by visual material to help you write a letter.

In Part 2, there are four tasks from which you **choose one** to write about. The range of tasks from which questions may be drawn includes an article, a report, a composition, a short story and a letter. The last question is based on the set books. These books remain on the list for about two years and you should contact UCLES or the UCLES local secretary in your area, if you wish to have the up-to-date list of background reading texts. If you decide to do the question on the set books, there will be two options from which you can choose **one** to write about.

Paper 3   Use of English

This paper consists of **five** parts and tests your control of English grammar, vocabulary and spelling. There are **65 questions** in total. The tasks include gapfilling exercises, sentence transformation, word formation and error correction.

Paper 4   Listening

This paper contains **four parts**. Each part contains a recorded text or texts and some questions including multiple choice, note-taking and matching. You hear each text twice. There is a total of **30 questions**.

Paper 5   Speaking

This paper consists of **four parts**. The standard test format is two candidates and two examiners. One examiner takes part in the conversation, the other examiner listens and gives marks. You will be given photographs and other visual material to look at and talk about. Sometimes you will talk with the other candidate, sometimes with the examiner and sometimes with both.

Marks and results

The total of marks in each paper is adjusted to 40 marks, so the five papers total 200 marks. Your overall FCE grade is based on the total score gained in all five papers. It is not necessary to achieve a satisfactory level in all five papers in order to pass the examination. Certificates are given to candidates who pass the examination with grade A, B or C. A is the highest. The minimum successful performance in order to achieve a grade C corresponds to about 60% of the total marks. D and E are failing grades. Your Statement of Results will include a graphical profile of your performance in each paper and show your relative performance in each one.

Further information

For more information about FCE, or any other UCLES examination write to:

UCLES EFL
1 Hills Road
Cambridge
CB1 2EU
England

Telephone: +44 1223 553311
Fax: +44 1223 460278.
e-mail: efl@ucles.org.uk
www.cambridge-efl.org.uk

Test 1

PAPER 1 READING (1 hour 15 minutes)

Part 1

You are going to read a newspaper article about air travel. Choose the most suitable summary sentence from the list **A–I** for each part (**1–7**) of the article. There is one extra summary sentence which you do not need to use. There is an example at the beginning (**0**).

Mark your answers **on the separate answer sheet**.

A	It is important to report missing luggage.
B	Airlines make special efforts to avoid errors.
C	Airlines sometimes blame travellers for lost luggage.
D	No airline is free from mistakes.
E	Plan ahead when travelling.
F	Unexpected events can result in luggage going missing.
G	No airport can guarantee the safe handling of luggage.
H	Busy airports are likely to have more problems.
I	Losing your luggage can be very inconvenient.

In case you lose your luggage

Alex McWhirter looks at airlines that lose bags.

0 | **I**

There is nothing more disappointing than arriving at an airport overseas to discover that your baggage has been left behind. At best you will have to put up with wearing the clothes you stand up in for hours or days, until the airline reunites you with your luggage. At worst, you may be in a different climate zone, thousands of miles from home and forced to wear wholly unsuitable clothes.

1

Although airlines rarely reveal how many cases they lose, it is a fact of life that sooner or later regular travellers will be parted from their luggage. Even the best airlines slip up from time to time, and it is impossible for any carrier to guarantee that a passenger's checked luggage will go on the same flight, particularly when a journey calls for one or more changes of aircraft.

2

The system works like this. Airlines insist on exaggerated check-in times (which require passengers to report to the airport at a given time before departure) designed to allow sufficient time for baggage to pass through the airport and be loaded on to the plane. Minimum connecting times (MCTs) are the shortest time it takes to transfer between two flights. These, too, are exaggerated to allow for baggage transfers.

3

In normal circumstances the system works well. But extra security checks at airports and problems with air traffic combine to cause delayed flights. All this can cause the baggage system to fail. Then there is the possibility of human error, or an accident in which the destination label is torn off.

4

These problems can become severe at large transfer airports, known as 'hubs', because of the large number of bags that are processed. Last year, for example, London's Heathrow airport handled more than 41 million passengers, of whom nine million were changing planes. British Airways alone handled two million transfer passengers at Heathrow, with most making the one-mile transfer between Terminal 1 (for Domestic and European flights) and Terminal 4 (for long-distance flights).

5

Even efficient transfer airports, such as Amsterdam, Copenhagen, Singapore and Zurich have their bad days. The risk of baggage being lost when changing planes is higher than average at certain airports. Even the United States has problems – Miami airport is well known for luggage going missing when transatlantic passengers make immediate connections for destinations in Latin America.

6

You should choose direct flights whenever possible and check in well before the official time. If a change of plane is unavoidable, or makes your flight less expensive, then try to fly the same airline throughout. Try to allow more connecting time by taking an earlier flight to the transfer airport, and make sure you label your luggage inside and out with your home and holiday addresses. Don't forget to include the flight numbers.

7

If, after all this, your luggage still goes missing, you must contact the appropriate airline official in the baggage hall and complete a *property irregularity report* (PIR). This must be done before leaving the airport.

Part 2

You are going to read an extract from a newspaper article. For Questions **8–14**, choose the answer (**A, B, C** or **D**) which you think fits best according to the text.

Mark your answers **on the separate answer sheet**.

A lot of advice is available for college leavers heading for their first job. In this article we consider the move to a second job. We are not concerned with those looking for a second temporary position while hunting for a permanent job. Nor are we concerned with those leaving an unsatisfactory job within the first few weeks. Instead, we will be dealing with those of you taking a real step on the career ladder, choosing a job to fit in with your ambitions now that you have learnt your way around, acquired some skills and have some idea of where you want to go.

What sort of job should you look for? Much depends on your long-term aim. You need to ask yourself whether you want to specialise in a particular field, work your way up to higher levels of responsibility or out of your current employment into a broader field.

Whatever you decide, you should choose your second job very carefully. You should be aiming to stay in it for two to three years.

26 This job will be studied very carefully when you send your letter of application for your next job. It should show evidence of serious career planning. Most important, it should extend you, develop you and give you increasing responsibility. Incidentally, if the travel bug is biting, now is the time to pack up and go. You can do temporary work for a while when you return, pick up where you left off and get the second job then. Future potential employers will be relieved to see that you have got it out of your system, and 34 are not likely to go off again.

Juliette Davidson spent her first year after leaving St. Aldate's College working for three solicitors. It was the perfect first job in that 'OK … they were very supportive people. I was gently introduced to the work, learnt my way round an office and improved my word processing skills. However, there was no scope for advancement. One day I gave in my notice, bought an air ticket and travelled for a year.'

Juliette now works as a Personal Assistant to Brenda Cleverdon, the Chief Executive of Business in the Community. 'In two and a half years I have become more able and my job has really grown,' she says. 'Right from the beginning my boss was very keen to develop me. My job title is the same as it was when I started but the duties have changed. From mainly typing and telephone work, I have progressed to doing most of the correspondence and budgets. I also have to deal with a variety of queries, coming from chairmen of large companies to people wanting to know how to start their own business. Brenda involves me in all her work but also gives me specific projects to do and events to organise.'

8 Who is intended to benefit from the advice given in the article?
   A students who have just finished their studies
   B people who are unhappy with their current job
   C those who are interested in establishing a career
   D people who change jobs regularly

9 According to the writer, why is the choice of your second job important?
   A It will affect your future job prospects.
   B It will last longer than your first job.
   C It will be difficult to change if you don't like it.
   D It should give you the opportunity to study.

10 'it' in line 26 refers to your
   A first job.
   B second job.
   C application.
   D career.

11 If you have a desire to travel, when does the writer suggest that you do it?
   A straight after you have left college
   B when you are unable to find a permanent job
   C after you have done some temporary work
   D between the first and second job

12 What is meant by 'you have got it out of your system' in line 34?
   A You have planned your career sensibly.
   B You are an experienced traveller.
   C You have satisfied your wish to travel.
   D You have learned to look after yourself.

13 How did Juliette Davidson benefit from the experience of her first job?
   A It was a good introduction to working in an office.
   B She met a variety of interesting people.
   C It enabled her to earn enough money to travel.
   D She learnt how to use a word processor.

14 In what way is Juliette's current job better than her first job?
   A She has a more impressive job title.
   B She now knows how to start her own business.
   C She has been able to extend her skills.
   D She is more involved in the community.

Part 3

You are going to read a newspaper article about chocolate. Eight sentences have been removed from the article. Choose from the sentences **A–I** the one which fits each gap (**15–21**). There is one extra sentence which you do not need to use. There is an example at the beginning (**0**).

Mark your answers **on the separate answer sheet**.

Bitter water hits the big time

Chocolate, which has its origins in South America, is now part of a multi-million pound worldwide business.

At Easter, British people spend over £230 million on chocolate. A massive eight per cent of all chocolate is bought at this time. | **0** | **I** | Although the large-scale industrial production of chocolate began in the last century, the cacao plant was first cultivated by the Aztec, Toltec and Mayan civilisations of Central America over three thousand years ago.

The cacao tree is an evergreen, tropical plant which is found in Africa, South and Central America, the West Indies and South-East Asia. The fruit of this tree is melon-sized and contains 20–40 seeds. | **15** | In English-speaking countries, they are often called cocoa beans. This is a misspelling from the 17th century when they were also called cacoa and cocao beans.

The Aztecs used cocoa beans as money. | **16** | This is from the word in the Aztec language, Nahuatl, meaning 'bitter water'. In Aztec times the chocolate drink was flavoured with spices and used on ceremonial occasions and for welcoming visitors. The Spanish found the drink more palatable mixed with cinnamon and sugar, but the recipe did not spread to the rest of Europe for another century. In the late 17th century, chocolate houses were set up in Europe's capital cities, where people gathered to drink chocolate.

| **17** | But in 1826, C J van Houten of the Netherlands invented chocolate powder. This was made by extracting most of the cocoa butter from the crushed beans.

The age of the chocolate bar as we know it began in 1847 when a Bristol company, Fry and Sons, combined cocoa butter with pure chocolate liquor and sugar to produce a solid block that you could eat. | **18** |

At the turn of the century, the British chocolate market was dominated by French companies. In 1879 the English company Cadbury even named their Birmingham factory Bournville (*ville* is the French word for town) in the hope that a little French glamour would rub off. But then came Cadbury's famous Dairy Milk bar which began life as Dairymaid in 1905. | **19** |

It seems that, for the time being at least, chocolate intake in Britain has stabilised at about four bars each week. **20** [ ] The latest marketing trick is the so-called 'extended line'. This is when the humble chocolate bar becomes an ice cream, a soft drink or a dessert, to tempt chocoholics who have grown tired of conventional snacks.

At the other end of the production process, cacao farmers are still feeling the effects of a crash in cocoa bean prices at the end of the 1980s. **21** [ ] Perhaps you could spare a thought for them as you munch your next chocolate bars.

A A Swiss company then introduced milk solids to the process which gave us milk chocolate.

B They also used them to make a drink called *xocoatl*.

C Until the last century, the chocolate drink was made from solid blocks of chocolate which had to be melted down in hot water.

D When dried they become cacao beans, which can be used to make chocolate.

E Clever advertising which associated it with the healthy qualities of milk from the English countryside quickly established the bar as a rival to the more decadent French brands.

F British manufacturers include up to 5 per cent vegetable fat in their chocolate, something forbidden elsewhere.

G As most cacao farmers operate on a very small scale, many were forced out of business.

H This has forced manufacturers to look for new ways to attract customers.

I Only at Christmas do people eat more of the cocoa-based foodstuffs.

Part 4

You are going to read a magazine article in which various women are interviewed. For Questions **22–35**, choose from the women (**A–F**). The women may be chosen more than once. When more than one answer is required, these may be given in any order. There is an example at the beginning (**0**).

Mark your answers **on the separate answer sheet**.

Which of the women states the following?

I don't remain interested in things for long.	**0**	F	
People I work with give me energy.	**22**		**23**
Being forced to do things uses up your energy.	**24**		
Doing things for the first time gives me energy.	**25**		
I have to make myself exercise.	**26**		
I enjoy behaving like a child.	**27**		
Certain kinds of people annoy me.	**28**		
It is important to me that others are interested in my work.	**29**		
You should use your energy carefully.	**30**		
Sometimes I lack energy at work.	**31**		

I like creating something from nothing.

| 32 | |

Being cheerful gives you energy.

| 33 | | | 34 | |

You should take every opportunity to have fun.

| 35 | |

WHERE I GET MY ENERGY

Emma Marsden asked six women who live life to the full to tell us how they do it.

| **A** | Jeanette Kupfermann |

Journalist and author: 'I think it's excitement. I've got to be doing something that's a challenge. If I'm absorbing something new and learning, I get tremendous energy. Anything to do with rhythm gives me energy, too – at the moment I'm learning flamenco dancing. Dance is wonderful, very expressive and energising. I think you can feel drained if you're bored, maybe feeling life is pointless. Being effective in the world – even in a small way – gives you energy.'

| **B** | Linda Kelsey |

Magazine editor: 'I have so much work to do but I enjoy it all – I love being at work, it isn't a chore. If you enjoy something, it doesn't make you feel low even though you may be feeling tired. I need a fair bit of sleep so when I do get it I feel really good. When I'm running at six hours' sleep a night, I feel a bit wet. I know exercise gives me energy, but it's finding the energy to do it! I do a yoga class once a week before work and I try to do a workout tape at home. But if I've done

exercise, my spirits rise amazingly. I get very low patches in the office between 3 and 5 in the afternoon and think it's probably good to eat something then.'

| **C** | Annie Nightingale |

Disc jockey: 'I don't eat healthily to get my energy – I think it's natural enthusiasm and being positive. I really can't stand people with negative attitudes. I'm quite naive – I think we should all enjoy our lives, grab the moment. Enjoyment comes first. You've got to achieve things and set yourself various goals. I enjoy what I do and the last two years have been very exciting. In my line of business there are lots of lively young people and you can't help being affected by that. I love tearing around the place on jobs, having a mad life. I'm very sociable. I enjoy taking photographs but I'm not sure if I'm good at it. I rush to get them processed and can't wait to get them back. I've also started writing words for imaginary songs – it's just for fun and it's a good release for my mind when I'm doing a lot of travelling.'

≫➤

D	Floella Benjamin

Author and children's TV presenter: 'My energy comes from things I do and enjoy. I believe in what I'm doing, both at work and at home with my family and I think that being positive about life helps. That's why I love working with kids, they give out so much and have an inbuilt resilience. Energy is like a natural chemical, triggered off by communicating with others – just try smiling at people and feel the thrill you get when they smile back. It's far better than feeling sorry for yourself. Although I try to eat healthily and don't smoke or drink, I don't have an exercise plan. The most energetic I get is running around with the kids and playing with them.'

E	Deborah Moggach

Author and playwright: 'What I love doing more than anything in the world is making a garden out of complete wasteland. I did that once. The garden was solid concrete – I smashed up all the concrete and dug in loads of soil. It was far better than any amount of workouts or tennis. The other thing that gives me energy is knowing that somebody wants to read what I'm writing – I find it difficult to write in a void. And I like sneaking into a farmer's land or a wood. If I'm found, I say "Oh, what a wonderful wood, I didn't know it was private property," and so on. I like it because it's childlike.'

F	Katherine Monblot

Therapist: 'I believe you must have an interest in and respect for what you do in life. I like to take risks and I get bored quickly, which keeps me motivated. Doing things you don't want to do wears you out. I used to be a member of various committees and resented the demands they made on my time. You only have a certain amount of energy, so direct it into the things that are most important to you.'

PAPER 2 WRITING (1 hour 30 minutes)

Part 1

You **must** answer this question.

1 You saw an advertisement for a house in the country and contacted the owner for more details, making the notes below. You and two friends have decided to book the house for two weeks in the summer. Since it is a large house, you would like to invite a fourth friend to join you.

Read the advertisement and the notes carefully. Then write a letter to a friend that you all know well, giving the necessary information about the house and the holiday and trying to persuade your friend to join you.

Devon countryside

House with swimming pool. Four bedrooms, large garden, use of four bicycles.

Plenty of local interest.
Some dates still available.

Tel. 0392-786-9596 for further details.

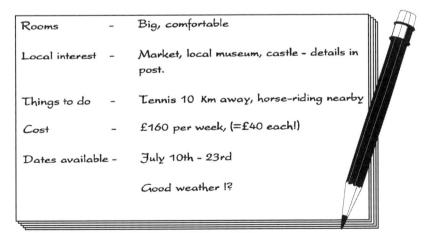

Rooms	-	Big, comfortable
Local interest	-	Market, local museum, castle – details in post.
Things to do	-	Tennis 10 Km away, horse-riding nearby
Cost	-	£160 per week, (=£40 each!)
Dates available –		July 10th - 23rd
		Good weather !?

Write a **letter** of between **120** and **180** words in an appropriate style on the next page. Do not write any addresses.

Question 1

Part 2

Write an answer to **one** of the Questions **2–5** in this part. Write your answer in **120–180** words in an appropriate style on the next page, putting the question number in the box.

2   An international publishing company intends to publish a book called *Influential People of the Twentieth Century*. The book will include short articles about politicians, writers, musicians, sports personalities and other people who have been important in some way. You have been invited to write a short article for this book about a person who has had either a good or bad influence on your country.

    Write your **article**.

3   The following comment was printed recently in a local newspaper:

    Much of what is taught in schools nowadays is a waste of students' time.

    Now your teacher has asked you to write a composition on this subject, with reference to your own learning experiences.

    Write your **composition**.

4   A group of foreign students is going to be staying in your town for a month. You have been asked to write a report for the group leader about eating out in your town. Describe the best places for the students to eat and drink in the area and explain why you think these places would be suitable for students from other countries.

    Write your **report**.

5   **Background reading texts**

    Answer **one** of the following two questions based on your reading of **one** of these five set books:

    A Passage to India – E. M. Forster   *Pygmalion* – G. B. Shaw
    Rebecca – Daphne du Maurier   *Brave New World* – Aldous Huxley
    Crime Never Pays – Oxford Bookworm Collection

    Your answer should contain enough detail to make it clear to someone who may not have read the book. Write the letter (**a**) or (**b**) as well as the number **5** in the question box, and the **title** of the book next to the box.

    Either   (a) What do you think are the **three** most surprising things in the book? Give reasons for your choices.

    Or   (b) If you could play a role in a film being made of the book, which role would you like to play and why?

Question	

....

....

....

....

....

....

....

....

....

....

....

....

....

....

....

....

....

....

....

....

....

....

....

....

....

....

....

PAPER 3   USE OF ENGLISH (1 hour 15 minutes)

Part 1

For Questions **1–15**, read the text below and decide which answer **A, B, C** or **D** best fits each space. There is an example at the beginning (**0**).
Mark your answers **on the separate answer sheet**.

Example:

0 A history   **B** age   **C** story   **D** legend

0	A	B	C	D

THE FIRST BICYCLE

The **(0)** ..... of the bicycle goes back more than 200 years. In 1791, Count de Sivrac
(1) ..... onlookers in a park in Paris as he showed off his two-wheeled invention, a
machine called the 'celerifere'. It was basically an **(2)** ..... version of a children's toy
which had been in **(3)** ..... for many years. Sivrac's 'celerifere' had a wooden frame,
made in the **(4)** ..... of a horse, which was mounted on a wheel at either end. To ride it,
you sat on a small seat, just like a modern bicycle, and pushed **(5)** ..... against the
(6) ..... with your legs – there were no pedals. It was impossible to steer a 'celerifere'
and it had no brakes, but despite these problems the invention very much **(7)** ..... to the
fashionable young men of Paris. Soon they were **(8)** ..... races up and down the streets.
Minor **(9)** ..... were common as riders attempted a final burst of **(10)** ..... . Controlling the
machine was difficult as the only way to change **(11)** ..... was to pull up the front of the
'celerifere' and **(12)** ..... it round while the front wheel was **(13)** ..... in the air.

'Celeriferes' were not popular for long, however, as the **(14)** ..... of no springs, no
steering and rough roads made riding them very uncomfortable. Even so, the wooden
'celerifere' was the **(15)** ..... of the modern bicycle.

1   **A**   delighted   **B**   cheered   **C**   appreciated   **D**   overjoyed

2   **A**   increased   **B**   enormous   **C**   extended   **D**   enlarged

3   **A**   use   **B**   play   **C**   operation   **D**   service

4   **A**   resemblance   **B**   shape   **C**   body   **D**   appearance

5   **A**   fast   **B**   deeply   **C**   heavily   **D**   hard

6   **A**   surface   **B**   ground   **C**   earth   **D**   floor

7   **A**   attracted   **B**   appealed   **C**   took   **D**   called

8   **A**   going   **B**   getting   **C**   holding   **D**   making

9   **A**   wounds   **B**   trips   **C**   injuries   **D**   breaks

10 **A**   velocity   **B**   energy   **C**   pace   **D**   speed

11 **A**   direction   **B**   route   **C**   heading   **D**   way

12 **A**   roll   **B**   drive   **C**   turn   **D**   revolve

13 **A**   cycling   **B**   circling   **C**   winding   **D**   spinning

14 **A**   mixture   **B**   link   **C**   combination   **D**   union

15 **A**   origin   **B**   design   **C**   model   **D**   introduction

Part 2

For Questions **16–30**, read the text below and think of the word which best fits each space. Use only **one** word in each space. There is an example at the beginning (**0**). Write your answers **on the separate answer sheet**.

Example: | **0** | in |

THE LAKE DISTRICT

One of the most beautiful parts of Britain is the Lake District. The Lake District is situated **(0)** .... the north-west of England and consists **(16)** .... high hills, mountains and, of course, lakes. In all there are sixteen lakes of **(17)** .... the largest is Lake Windermere.

Over the years many writers have **(18)** .... associated with this region but there can be no doubt that the most famous of **(19)** .... was William Wordsworth (1770–1850), **(20)** .... was born and lived almost the whole of his life there. He had close connections **(21)** .... the village of Grasmere, **(22)** .... he lived **(23)** .... some thirteen years. He loved **(24)** .... particular part of England and many of his poems speak of the joy he felt when surrounded by beautiful countryside.

Every year more than fourteen million people **(25)** .... Britain and abroad visit the Lake District to enjoy the fresh air and the scenery. Some go to walk in the mountains while others sail boats on the lakes **(26)** .... simply sit admiring the magnificent views. Unfortunately, the region **(27)** .... becoming a victim of **(28)** .... own success in attracting visitors; **(29)** .... many people come to the Lake District that they threaten to destroy the peace and quiet which many **(30)** .... searching for there.

Part 3

For Questions **31–40**, complete the second sentence so that it has a similar meaning to the first sentence, using the word given. **Do not change the word given**. You must use between two and five words, including the word given.

Here is an example (**0**).

Example:

0   My brother is too young to drive a car.

    not

    My brother .... drive a car.

    The gap can be filled by the words 'is not old enough to' so you write:

0	is not old enough to

Write **only the missing words** on the separate answer sheet.

---

31   Ballet doesn't interest Sonia.
    interested

    Sonia .... ballet.

32   Visitors to the zoo are not allowed to feed the animals.
    must

    The animals .... by visitors to the zoo.

33   John had not been to London before.
    visit

    It .... London.

34   'I'll see you later Anne,' he said.
    told

    He .... see her later.

35   There were more students in school in 1992 than in 1991.
    as

    There were .... in school in 1991 as in 1992.

36 When I was in the department store, someone thought I was a shop assistant.
me

When I was in the department store, someone .... a shop assistant.

37 I wonder how she learnt to speak English so well.
like

I .... know how she learnt to speak English so well.

38 Although he can't swim himself, Dan is very keen that his children should learn.
unable

Despite .... himself, Dan is very keen that his children should learn.

39 I am totally convinced that our team will win.
chance

In my opinion, there .... our team losing.

40 It's a good thing you wrote the letter or we wouldn't have known what happened.
you

We wouldn't have known what happened .... that letter.

Part 4

For Questions **41–55**, read the text below and look carefully at each line. Some of the lines are correct, and some have a word which should not be there.
If a line is correct, put a tick (✓) by the number **on the separate answer sheet**. If a line has a word which should **not** be there, write the word **on the separate answer sheet**. There are two examples at the beginning (**0** and **00**).

0	✓

Examples:

00	than

MEETING A FRIEND

0	Last year I had a most enjoyable experience when I met somebody I
00	had been writing to for over than seven years. When I was about twelve
41	years old one of the teachers at school asked if anyone had wanted to
42	have an English pen-friend. I had recently begun learning English and
43	as I was finding it being rather difficult I thought this might help me.
44	A few weeks much later the teacher gave me the address of a boy who
45	lived in Leeds. We began to write to each other straight away and
46	usually exchanged the letters about twice a month. We often wrote that
47	we would like to meet but, unfortunately, this was never possible.
48	However, last year I was sent on a two-week course in London by my
49	firm. There was a great deal of my work to do and I did not have much
50	time free but on the second weekend my friend came to see me. I
51	wondered about if we would really like each other when we met.
52	Fortunately, there was absolutely nothing all to worry about; we had been
53	writing for so long time that it was like meeting an old friend. We had
54	a meal together and spent the whole of the day while talking about our
55	shared interests. I hope we will be able to meet ourselves again soon.

Part 5

For Questions **56–65**, read the text below. Use the word given in capitals at the end of each line to form a word that fits in the space in the same line. There is an example at the beginning (**0**).
Write your answers **on the separate answer sheet**.

Example:

0	invention

WEATHER FORECASTING

Before the **(0)** *invention* of instruments to measure weather conditions,	**INVENT**
people relied on their own **(56)** ..... of the wind and sky as well as the	**OBSERVE**
(57) ..... of birds and animals in connection with different types of	**BEHAVE**
weather. Many rhymes that have an **(58)** ..... with the weather have	**ASSOCIATE**
become popular over the centuries. In the short term, a **(59)** ..... like	**SAY**
'red sky in the morning, sailor's warning', often proves to be **(60)** ..... accurate.	**SURPRISE**
However, it is very **(61)** ..... that next year's summer can be predicted	**LIKELY**
from this year's winter. Such predictions can't be considered **(62)**	**USE**
in precise weather forecasting. **(63)** ..... of this can be found in past records.	**PROVE**
Nowadays, all aspects of the weather such as hours of **(64)**	**SUN**
and rainfall are observed on a **(65)**..... basis by meteorological	**DAY**
stations with specialised equipment.	

PAPER 4 LISTENING (approximately 40 minutes)

Part 1

You will hear people talking in eight different situations. For Questions **1–8**, choose the best answer, **A, B** or **C**.

---

1 You hear a young man talking to his friend about a film.
What is his opinion of the film?

   A   It was too long.

   B   The acting was poor.

   C   There was too much violence.

                                                        1

2 You hear part of an interview with a man on the radio.
What is the man talking about?

   A   shopping

   B   gardening

   C   painting

                                                        2

3 You hear a man talking about his job.
Where does he work?

   A   in a hotel

   B   in a travel agent's

   C   in a shop

                                                        3

4 You hear Jessica telling a friend about a trip.
Why is she going to Japan?

   A   to do some painting

   B   to learn Japanese

   C   to study Japanese art

                                                        4

5 In a hospital waiting room, you hear this conversation.
What is the man doing?

    A making a complaint

    B expressing approval

    C making a suggestion

                                                                     5

6 You hear some friends talking.
How does the woman feel?

    A worried

    B annoyed

    C disappointed

        6

7 You overhear two people talking in a café.
What is the relationship between them?

    A They belong to the same club.

    B They are students together.

    C They work for the same company.

        7

8 You hear part of a radio programme on the subject of films.
What is special about the music in John Hunt's film?

    A It holds your attention.

    B It follows the action.

    C It stays in your memory.

        8

Part 2

You will hear part of a nature programme for young people in Britain. For Questions
9–18, fill in the missing information.

Nature Notes

NATURAL HISTORY MUSEUM

best time to visit: | 9 |

museum also operates the | 10 |

popular attraction there is called the | 11 |

'ROCKWATCH' PROJECT

aim is for youngsters to become | 12 | rock collectors

youngsters can attend events called | 13 |

SOCIETY FOR THE PROTECTION OF BIRDS

name of competition: | 14 |

article must be about the | 15 |

EDINBURGH ZOO: OPEN DAY

begins with | 16 |

ends with | 17 | in a hotel

price includes | 18 | to take away

Part 3

You will hear five people talking about experiences connected with school. For Questions **19–23**, choose from the list **A–F** what each speaker says about his or her school days. Use the letters only once. There is one extra letter which you do not need to use.

A   I played a variety of sports.

Speaker 1 | | **19**

B   I wanted to develop practical skills.

Speaker 2 | | **20**

C   I wanted to study harder.

Speaker 3 | | **21**

D   I was helped by a particular teacher.

Speaker 4 | | **22**

E   I had a problem with another pupil.

Speaker 5 | | **23**

F   I was lazy.

Part 4

You will hear part of a radio interview with a famous Australian novelist, Dorothy Shields. For Questions **24–30**, decide which of the statements are TRUE and which are FALSE. Write **T** for True or **F** for False in the boxes provided.

_____

24 She has only written about part of her life. | 24

25 She wants to keep her friends' secrets. | 25

26 She failed to stop someone else writing her life story. | 26

27 She laughs when people write untrue things about her. | 27

28 She no longer destroys unsatisfactory work. | 28

29 Not many people liked her first published novel. | 29

30 She was amazed when the publisher accepted her novel. | 30

PAPER 5   SPEAKING (approximately 14 minutes)

You take the Speaking test with another candidate, referred to here as your partner. There are two examiners. One will speak to you and your partner and the other will just be listening. Both examiners will award marks.

Part 1 (3 minutes)
The examiner asks you and your partner questions about yourselves. You may be asked about things like 'your home town', 'your interests', 'your career plans', etc.

Part 2 (4 minutes)
The examiner gives you two photographs and asks you to talk about them for about one minute. The examiner then asks your partner a question about your photographs and your partner responds briefly.

Then the examiner gives your partner two different photographs. Your partner talks about these photographs for about one minute. This time the examiner asks you a question about your partner's photographs and you respond briefly.

Part 3 (3 minutes)
The examiner asks you and your partner to talk together. You may be asked to discuss something, solve a problem or perhaps come to a decision about something. For example, you might be asked to decide the best way to use some rooms in a language school. The examiner gives you a picture to help you but does not join in the conversation.

Part 4 (4 minutes)
The examiner asks some further questions, which lead to a more general discussion of what you have talked about in Part 3.

Test 2

PAPER 1   READING (1 hour 15 minutes)

Part 1

You are going to read an information sheet about a model village. Choose the most suitable heading from the list **A–I** for each part (**1–7**) of the information sheet. There is one extra heading which you do not need to use. There is an example at the beginning (**0**).

Mark your answers **on the separate answer sheet**.

A	High quality sets new standards
B	Some important instructions
C	Preparing the ground
D	A whole village reproduced
E	Choosing the best materials
F	Difficult growing conditions
G	Open to suggestions
H	Typical village features
I	Land nobody wanted

WELCOME TO THE MODEL VILLAGE

0	I

When you first enter the Model Village it is hard to imagine that a few short years ago this was a piece of waste ground, flat and completely overgrown with brambles. For years it had been considered a worthless piece of land. The careful planning and hard work of one man, supported unfailingly by his wife, turned this piece of ground into the masterpiece you see today.

1	

Many thousands of tons of soil and clay were moved during the construction of the village to change a flat site into the sculptured landscape you see today. Although bulldozers and digging machines helped to transform the land, it also involved an enormous amount of hard labour. Once shaped, approximately 1,000 tonnes of top soil were brought in and laid over it to create the lawns, flower-beds and rockeries.

2	

In the creation of the Model Village, hundreds of trees and shrubs were planted. These had to be carefully selected for the area. Only those plants which were able to tolerate the salt-laden atmosphere so close to the sea could be used. They also had to stand up to the severe winter gales in this very exposed position. Most of the plants were provided by local garden centres but some came from as far away as Canada and New Zealand.

3	

The whole village was conceived by Colin Sims and the models, over 100, were individually made by him over a period of nine years from when the village was first opened, in 1972. The models are constructed from a variety of materials - stone, concrete, specially treated wood and plastics - to withstand all kinds of weather. Initially, Colin had to seek considerable assistance from experts who explained to him how various materials would stand up to years of changing weather. But very soon he became an expert himself.

4	

You will soon notice that a constant scale has been strictly adhered to and that attention has been paid to even the smallest detail on the models. This has been achieved by patience and the development of unique construction techniques. The Model Village has proved to be a very popular attraction and is noted for its high standard of workmanship and maintenance. The techniques used to construct such true-to-life models have since been used in other model villages around England and have even been included in some courses at colleges where modelling can be studied.

5	

All model buildings you will see in the village portray traditional British architectural forms and are not based strictly on one particular place or structure. One of the most impressive buildings is the Manor House. This is a typical 13th century stone structure with a brick tower and stone walls. It is based on the style of manor houses commonly found in the West Country. As you walk round the village you will also notice the Castle, St Mary's Church, a zoo and mini golf course, the latter being the most recent addition to the village.

6	

We ask you to keep to the paths during your visit and not to touch any of the models; a slip on your part can result in hours of repair work for us. Photography is allowed from the pathways only. Dogs are welcome on a short lead. To further your enjoyment of the Model Village, you will see buttons mounted in front of some of the working models. Press these and you will make the models operate.

7	

At the end of your visit we would welcome any comments you might have. New models are being planned all the time and any new ideas will help us design a more varied and interesting display. We would also like to know which models, if any, you thought were not up to the standard of the rest of the village. We are continually replacing and updating the models and we need to know which ones require some attention. We hope you enjoy your visit and we look forward to seeing you another day. Don't forget to tell your friends about it.

Part 2

You are going to read a short story. For Questions **8–15**, choose the answer
(**A, B, C** or **D**) which you think fits best according to the text.

Mark your answers **on the separate answer sheet**.

HAPPY HUNTING GROUND

We're 'animal people' who enjoy the company of all kinds of creatures. Consider this typical chain of events, leading to total confusion, which began one afternoon. My daughter telephoned me at work with the news that she had found a wonderful pine snake.

'Can we keep him?' she cried. I said 'Yes, but only overnight.' We had set up a special tank for just such passers-through, overnight being long enough to admire and look them up in our well-used natural history book.

I was late getting home. I hurriedly put a pot on to boil just as screams of 'Oh, Mother! Help! Do something!' came from my sons' bedroom. I leapt to it.

The crisis involved Domino the cat and Bianca the white mouse given to me as a Mother's Day present. (I've
23   heard that some mothers get perfume.) Domino, with mouse feet waving from his jaws, ran round and round the bedroom that was crowded with furniture and children.

Looking for a way out so he could enjoy his catch, Domino had so far avoided the forest of waving arms. I threw myself into the confusion and promptly tripped over something or someone to find myself on the floor.

As I thought about dropping my full weight on Domino when he next came past, my eyes locked on the snake. It had escaped - or, more correctly, was escaping. It was pouring itself up and out and off the table and all over the floor. I crouched like a rabbit at the approach of its bullish head, and long powerful body.

The snake and I were now both being jumped over by cat/mouse/kids in a screaming, leaping, hissing mass - the snake striking at every moment, the dog barking wildly.

The pot boiled over in the kitchen and I raced to shut off the gas, returning to the battle with new strength. This time I successfully captured Domino by the tail, and pulled the small, damp and
60   miraculously uninjured mouse from his growling jaws. Incidentally, the same mouse was caught by the same cat three more times during its lifetime, but eventually died of old age.

Encouraged by my success with the cat, I looked the snake over for weak points. It didn't have any. In the end, I sat on the floor like a snake-charmer, rocking backwards and forwards, but without a flute. Gradually the snake relaxed enough to drop its head on to its piled-up body, but its eyes still shone with suspicion. I eventually ever-so-slowly eased my hands beneath the piled-up snake and gradually raised myself to a kneeling position, then I stood up and walked to the very end of the garden where I gave the snake the choice of living happily ever after on the garden shed by pointing it in the direction of a handy tree.

But when I finally gathered enough courage to release the snake's head - fully expecting it to swing instantly around to crush my face in its powerful jaws - it slid away from the tree and up over my shoulders where, like a colourful leathery shawl, it gave every sign of making itself comfortable for the winter.

We stood in the gathering dusk, four young children, Mum and the snake. DJ, my eldest, broke the heavy silence with a scientific explanation: 'You know what it is, Mum? You're nice and fat and warm, and the shed isn't.' I had the children gather at the snake's tail end and gently encourage it to move on. Slowly and unwillingly it did so. Without a backward glance, the snake travelled smoothly up the wall to disappear over the now night-shadowed roof.

As the last tiny bit of tail disappeared from our property, three-year old Clay sighed and said it for all of us: 'Boy, that was one big snake!'

8   Why did the children start shouting?
   A   They were arguing about what to do.
   B   The cat had eaten the mouse.
   C   The snake had frightened them.
   D   They wanted their mother to save the mouse.

9   What does the writer really mean when she says 'I've heard that some mothers get perfume' (line 23)?
   A   She would not be surprised to receive perfume.
   B   She sometimes received perfume.
   C   She thinks perfume is a strange present.
   D   She would quite like to receive perfume.

10   When did she realise the snake was escaping?
   A   when she arrived in the bedroom
   B   as she lay on the floor
   C   when she tripped over it
   D   as she grabbed the cat

11   What does she mean when she says she was 'encouraged' by her success with the cat (line 60)?
   A   She now had the confidence to deal with the snake.
   B   The cat was no longer a threat.
   C   The snake no longer seemed so strong.
   D   The children were pleased with what she'd done.

12   How did she get the snake out of the house?
   A   She frightened it.
   B   She sent it to sleep.
   C   She chased it away.
   D   She carried it.

13   Where did the snake move to instead of the tree?
   A   up the garden wall
   B   onto the writer's shoulders
   C   onto the roof of the shed
   D   into the garden

14   The snake finally left the garden when the writer
   A   used her hands to give it a push.
   B   let go of its head.
   C   got her children to help.
   D   stood up quickly.

15   Why was the story written?
   A   to warn
   B   to amuse
   C   to instruct
   D   to advise

Part 3

You are going to read a newspaper article about dolphins. Eight sentences have been removed from the article. Choose from the sentences **A–I** the one which fits each gap (**16–22**). There is one extra sentence which you do not need to use. There is an example at the beginning (**0**).

Mark your answers **on the separate answer sheet**.

Behind the dolphin's smile

People love dolphins. We rush to look at them in seaside marinas, films and TV programmes. Yet according to the Whale and Dolphin Conservation Society their plight is desperate. Mark Simmonds reports on the decline of the species.

Dolphins hold a special place in our affections. They are among the most intelligent animals we know, they are sensitive to human emotions, and they allow us to dream of wonderful freedom out in the wild seas. | **0** | **I** | First there was *Flipper*, and now there's Darwin, the star of *Seaquest*. However, these happy portrayals hide the reality of life for dolphins in the polluted and overfished seas of the late twentieth century.

The population of North Sea harbour porpoises (one kind of dolphin) is estimated to have been reduced by up to 89,000. You may expect such popular animals to be protected by law and taken care of in special marine reserves. | **16** |

Forty different kinds of dolphins are recognised worldwide. In the waters of northern Europe, the greatest number of dolphins are the striped, the common, the bottlenose dolphins, and the smaller harbour porpoise. | **17** | They are normally seen only in small groups, flashing quickly past ships, and we know very little about them.

| **18** | Bottlenoses are particularly social and used to be found on the Channel coast and in river mouths in Britain, including the Thames. Resident populations can nowadays be found only in the Moray Firth in Scotland and Cardigan Bay in Wales, and the skin injuries found on the few that still remain indicate that they are suffering from stress.

The complicated habits of the dolphins make it difficult to decide on the exact reasons for this reduction in numbers. The overfishing which is dramatically reducing the world's fish stocks and which is threatening to destroy local fishing industries, also threatens porpoises and dolphins. This is because porpoises have to find their food within a limited time. **19** [   ]

They are also in danger of getting caught in fishermen's nets which are thought to be invisible to them. In many modern fishing methods, huge nets are left to float or are pulled at great speed through the sea. **20** [   ] Marks, ropes and cuts on their bodies show that the main cause of death was the fact that they had been caught by such nets.

21 [   ] One example is what happens with pesticides: these poisons are soluble in fat, which means that the dolphins can digest them and they can build up in their bodies. The females then produce milk that is rich in pesticides, thus passing the poison in a concentrated fashion on to their young. There is already one recorded case of a young dolphin being poisoned and killed by its mother's milk.

But perhaps the most controversial threat to dolphins is the one posed by human disturbance. **22** [   ] In the sea, noise pollution - from ships, oil wells and so on - is transmitted four times more efficiently than in the air. This may disturb the dolphins in ways that we do not yet understand.

A   Dolphins live in groups and receive information about much of their world through sound.

B   If fish in one area are removed by fishing, they may not survive long enough to find food elsewhere.

C   In recent years, hundreds of dead dolphins have been washed up on the beaches of France and Cornwall.

D   Special dolphin shows have therefore always been extremely popular.

E   Waste and other substances found in the sea can be stored in the bodies of dolphins.

F   This is not the case, however, and the lack of plans to look after them may become one of the biggest wildlife disasters of our times.

G   The large grey bottlenoses and harbour porpoises, on the other hand, were once a common sight near to European coasts.

H   The first two generally live far out in the open sea.

I   This love affair has been encouraged by TV.

Part 4

You are going to read a magazine article about careers advice. For Questions **23–35**, choose from the people (**A–D**). The people may be chosen more than once. When more than one answer is required, these may be given in any order. There is an example at the beginning (**0**).

Mark your answers **on the separate answer sheet**.

Which of the people suggest the following?

A	THE WRITER
B	DONNA LANEY
C	JULIET GREENE
D	AMANDA MARGETTS

I wasn't keen on what was suggested.	**0**	D
I couldn't see how the tests could provide the necessary information.	**23**	
I have a different attitude since making some changes.	**24**	
I discovered a skill I didn't know I had.	**25**	
Careers advice proved me right about my choice of job.	**26**	
I would have made my career change without advice.	**27**	
I could have got the same advice from people I already know.	**28**	
I found my performance in some tests a bit disappointing.	**29**	
Circumstances gave me the chance to reconsider my career choice.	**30**	
I have recommended a particular careers service to others.	**31**	
I heard things I was already aware of.	**32**	

I'm about to make a major change. | 33 |

I felt under pressure in the tests. | 34 |

One of the techniques helped me a lot. | 35 |

Careers Advice

You're not happy in your job at the moment, but you don't know how to change?
Kitty Doherty *gives some good advice.*

The answer for more and more people who want to change their job is to turn to a careers adviser. You will be asked to write a brief history of yourself and then sit through a number of tests known as 'psychometrics'. A summary of the findings is then given and various careers are suggested, as well as the possible retraining needed.

I decided to try out Career Analysts, one of the largest organisations giving career advice. Taking the careers test was like being back in my science exams. I was with a group of about ten people and we were answering questions against the clock. I had to remember that it wasn't about passing or failing. It was hard to see how the psychometrics would give an accurate picture of me. They involved things like picking out mistakes in lists of names and numbers and matching up similar shapes in a set.

I then had a long chat with an adviser and from this, plus the results of the test, he produced a report giving his observations and recommendations. I agreed with most of the adviser's conclusions, though I was a little dismayed to find out that I had done quite badly in the scientific, technical and practical tests. I am sure that a lot of sick people are glad that I never became a nurse. It was reassuring, though, to be told that I had made the correct decisions as far as journalism was concerned.

Rethinking your career needn't involve a massive change of direction. Last March, after working as a marketing manager with a large insurance company for five years, **Donna Laney**, 25, lost her job. Her friends suggested she go to Career Analysts for help. 'Losing my job was the perfect opportunity for me to take a step back and look at my career to date. I wanted to re-examine the skills and interests I have,' says Donna. Some of the results were surprising. 'I hadn't realised that I had such a gift for design. But in the end I had to balance the cost of retraining in design against my financial commitments,' she says. Other suggestions were put forward, such as taking a year off and working in the Far East.

'I decided to use the skills I already had and move into something more suited to me than insurance. I am now working as a Public Relations officer. I am sure I would have got to this point without Career Analysts but they helped me realise, objectively and

⋙➤

independently, what I definitely wanted to do. I have sent half a dozen friends there, who are all happy with the service.'

There are those who feel that they definitely would not have got to that point without help. A visit to Career Counselling Services led 26-year-old **Juliet Greene** to make some life-changing decisions. 'After working for a major bank for six years, I decided my job was dull and I needed a new challenge. I had no idea what I wanted to do so I went to Career Counselling Services with a completely open mind. I took the tests, which showed I was interested in sciences,' she says. 'I had four sessions with an adviser. The third session was taped, which I found very useful, as you forget many of the things you say. After the fourth meeting, having listened carefully to what the results of the tests were telling me, I made the decision that I wanted to do geology and I plan to start a

degree course in it later this year. I think that the advice given by Career Counselling Services was well worth the fee. I'm a lot happier now and far more positive.'

However, careers advice doesn't work for everyone. **Amanda Margetts**, a 24-year-old sales representative, says: 'I had reached a stage in my career where I didn't know where to go. I thought a careers adviser might suggest something I had never thought of. Although I was given a host of new ideas, I rejected them as they either required a substantial drop in salary or considerable retraining. I wasn't told anything about myself that I didn't know,' she says. 'You have to provide the adviser with an enormous amount of personal information and I just felt that if I had told a friend the same thing, they would have given me similar advice.'

PAPER 2   WRITING (1 hour 30 minutes)

Part 1

You **must** answer this question.

1   You help to organise social events at an international student college. Read the note from
      your colleague, Tony, and the extract from the college regulations. Then write to the
      Principal of the college asking permission to have a party and giving her some information
      about the organisation of the party.

Could you write to Ms Henderson - she's now the Principal of the college - and ask
permission for us to have a party at the end of term? Remember there were some
complaints from the neighbours and the college cleaners after the last party, so you
will have to persuade her there won't be any problems this time! These are the
decisions we have made so far:

Date	-	31 March
Time	-	8 pm - 11.30 pm
Place	-	College canteen
Music	-	Disco
Food and drink	-	Amanda
Decorations	-	Noriko

Thanks,

Tony

COLLEGE REGULATIONS

Parties

Parties may be held in the College provided that:

-   an application is made, in writing, giving **full details** to the Principal of the
    college at least 14 days before the suggested date of the party
-   there is no noise after midnight
-   all rooms used for the party are left clean and tidy.

Write a **letter** of between **120** and **180** words in an appropriate style on the next page. Do
not write any addresses.

Question 1

Part 2

Write an answer to **one** of the Questions **2–5** in this part. Write your answer in **120–180** words in an appropriate style on the next page, putting the question number in the box.

2   A close relative of yours got married last weekend. Your cousin, who lives abroad, was not able to come to the wedding. Write a letter to your cousin, describing the wedding. Describe the whole day **and** include some details about the people who came to the wedding celebrations. Do not write any addresses.

   Write your **letter**.

3   You have decided to enter a short story competition. The competition rules say that the story must begin with the following words:

   I will never forget my first day at . . .

   Write your **story** for the competition.

4   Your college magazine has invited you to suggest helpful ways of remembering new vocabulary in English. Write an article for the magazine, giving your suggestions.

   Write your **article**.

5   **Background reading texts**
   Answer **one** of the following two questions based on your reading of **one** of these five set books:

   A Passage to India – E. M. Forster   *Pygmalion* – G. B. Shaw
   Rebecca – Daphne du Maurier   *Brave New World* – Aldous Huxley
   Crime Never Pays – Oxford Bookworm Collection

   Your answer should contain enough detail to make it clear to someone who may not have read the book. Write the letter **(a)** or **(b)** as well as the number **5** in the question box, and the **title** of the book next to the box.

   Either   **(a)**   A new edition of the book is being prepared. Imagine that you can ask an artist to draw **two** pictures to illustrate the cover. Describe the pictures which you would ask the artist to draw and explain why you chose them.

   Or   **(b)**   In your opinion, which character changes most in the book or one of the short stories?

Question	

....

....

....

....

....

....

....

....

....

....

....

....

....

....

....

....

....

....

....

....

....

....

....

....

....

....

....

....

....

PAPER 3   USE OF ENGLISH (1 hour 15 minutes)

Part 1

For Questions **1–15**, read the text below and decide which answer **A, B, C** or **D** best fits each space. There is an example at the beginning **(0)**.
Mark your answers **on the separate answer sheet**.

Example:

0 A taken   **B** brought   **C** shown   **D** visited

0	A	B	C	D
	<u> </u>			

ZOOS

Many people remember being **(0)** ..... to the zoo as a child. They remember especially the excitement of **(1)** ..... seeing animals for the first **(2)** ..... , when before they had only read about them in books or seen them on television. However, there is **(3)** ..... discussion today about the future of zoos and what their role should be.

Supporters of zoos claim that they have an educational **(4)** ..... and represent a good way for people of **(5)** ..... ages to learn more about the natural world. Also, zoos provide **(6)** ..... for important research and frequently **(7)** ..... scientists to help save those animals which are becoming **(8)** ..... rare in the wild.

Opponents, however, criticise zoos for a number of reasons. Firstly, they say that it is **(9)** ..... to keep animals in cages. Even in the best zoos, animals may **(10)** ..... because the places in which they have to live are both restricted and **(11)** ..... . This can cause them to **(12)** ..... stress and can affect their health. Secondly, they believe that money would be **(13)** ..... spent on protecting animals in their **(14)** ..... environment. Finally, opponents **(15)** ..... out that most people nowadays can see well-made nature documentaries on television and that this is a much more valuable experience than going to a zoo.

1   A   actually   B   genuinely   C   positively   D   truly

2   A   moment   B   event   C   occasion   D   time

3   A   deep   B   considerable   C   large   D   important

4   A   activity   B   function   C   situation   D   occupation

5   A   several   B   both   C   all   D   every

6   A   ways   B   reasons   C   methods   D   opportunities

7   A   make   B   arrange   C   allow   D   let

8   A   completely   B   increasingly   C   totally   D   greatly

9   A   violent   B   severe   C   heavy   D   cruel

10 A   suffer   B   injure   C   fail   D   hurt

11 A   designed   B   manufactured   C   artificial   D   false

12 A   experience   B   have   C   create   D   bear

13 A   further   B   rather   C   better   D   more

14 A   standard   B   daily   C   typical   D   natural

15 A   pick   B   point   C   show   D   speak

Part 2

For Questions **16–30**, read the text below and think of the word which best fits each space. Use only **one** word in each space. There is an example at the beginning **(0)**. Write your answers **on the separate answer sheet**.

Example: | **0** | by |

COFFEE

Coffee is made from the beans that grow in the fruits of the coffee plant. There are usually two beans in each fruit and harvesting is done **(0)** .... hand.

The word 'coffee' derives from the Arabic 'qahwah', a word **(16)** .... was originally used for wine, but which came to mean coffee. Coffee beans **(17)** .... to be chewed before it was discovered that they **(18)** .... be boiled with water **(19)** .... make a drink.

Coffee drinking began in Arab countries in the 14th century and did not **(20)** .... common in Europe **(21)** .... the 17th century. At **(22)** .... , coffee was sold by chemists, but it **(23)** .... little impact until the first coffee shop opened and instructions about **(24)** .... to roast and grind the coffee were published.

In London, the first coffee houses – places **(25)** .... people met, drank coffee and talked – opened in 1652. In 1657 the King tried to close them **(26)** .... they were reported to disturb 'the peace and quiet of the nation'. They did indeed have a great influence **(27)** .... political and commercial life. Several modern banks and other financial institutions have **(28)** .... origins in these coffee houses.

By the end of the 19th century, demand **(29)** .... coffee had grown and there were a great many plantations in tropical Africa. Today, **(30)** .... world's largest producers are Brazil, Colombia and the Ivory Coast.

Part 3

For Questions **31–40**, complete the second sentence so that it has a similar meaning to the first sentence, using the word given. **Do not change the word given**. You must use between two and five words, including the word given.

Here is an example **(0)**.

Example:

0 My brother is too young to drive a car.

   not

   My brother .... drive a car.

   The gap can be filled by the words 'is not old enough to' so you write:

0	is not old enough to

Write **only the missing words** on the separate answer sheet.

---

31 Luisa was the only one who didn't enjoy the film.
   apart

   Everybody .... Luisa.

32 They're going to demolish that old power station.
   pulled

   That old power station .... down.

33 My sister began to learn Russian five years ago.
   learning

   My sister .... five years.

34 'Do not answer the phone, Rebecca!' said Mrs Miniver.
   not

   Mrs Miniver .... answer the phone.

35 The trip to Chicago was cheaper than I had expected.
   as

   The trip to Chicago .... I had expected.

36 My watch was so badly damaged that it wasn't worth keeping.
point

My watch was so badly damaged that .... keeping it.

37 I expect you were exhausted after your long journey.
been

You .... exhausted after your long journey.

38 It was unfair that the gymnast was given such low marks.
deserve

The gymnast .... given such low marks.

39 This bottle is completely empty.
left

There's .... bottle.

40 My uncle did not learn to drive until he was forty.
when

My uncle .... to drive.

Part 4

For Questions **41–55**, read the text below and look carefully at each line. Some of the lines are correct, and some have a word which should not be there.
If a line is correct, put a tick **(✓)** by the number **on the separate answer sheet**. If a line has a word which should **not** be there, write the word **on the separate answer sheet**. There are two examples at the beginning (**0** and **00**).

Examples:

0	one

00	✓

SPORTS FANS

0   For some people, sport is the most important one thing in their lives. In

00   a great many countries all over the world, football, for example, is

41   followed with enormous passion by millions of people. For such as fans,

42   football is much more than just a game – it has a big effect on their

43   emotions. If the team that they support it wins, they are extremely happy

44   but if it should lose, they can become extremely depressed, angry and

45   even go aggressive. They regard the players in their team as heroes if they

46   play well but they quickly change their opinion if they start to play so badly.

47   In some places they celebrate all the night if their team wins an important

48   game and some fans even they give their children the names of their

49   favourite players. The fortunes of a team can affect to the mood of a whole

50   town or country – if it has won a big competition, production in

51   factories can increase because of the workers are happy. Some people find

52   this attitude to sport ridiculous. They cannot understand that why it is

53   possible for adults to get so much excited about a group of people kicking a

54   ball around a field. They think that these kind fans are childish and as far as

55   they are concerned, fans who like that take sport far too seriously.

Part 5

For Questions **56–65**, read the text below. Use the word given in capitals at the end of each line to form a word that fits in the space in the same line. There is an example at the beginning **(0)**. Write your answers **on the separate answer sheet**.

Example:

0	effective

EXCHANGE VISITS

The most **(0)** *effective* way of learning a language is by living in the   **EFFECT**

country concerned, but parents should think **(56)** ..... before they   **CARE**

send their children abroad. Although some **(57)** ..... arrange visits   **ORGANISE**

for children as young as ten, the **(58)** ..... of them won't be ready   **MAJOR**

to stay away from home and deal with **(59)** ..... differences until they   **CULTURE**

are in their teens. Even then they will need a basic **(60)** ..... of the   **KNOW**

language and some experience of foreign travel before they go.

Exchange visits are a good way for **(61)** ..... to improve their   **TEENS**

language skills. It is a good idea for them to exchange **(62)** .....   **CORRESPOND**

before the visits. Host families should not feel any **(63)** .....   **OBLIGE**

to provide an extensive programme of **(64)** ..... . It is more   **ENTERTAIN**

important to make the guest feel welcome.

Travel can **(65)** ..... the mind, and exchange visits give young people   **BROAD**

experience of a different way of life as well as a different language.

PAPER 4   LISTENING (approximately 40 minutes)

Part 1

You will hear people talking in eight different situations. For Questions **1–8**, choose the best answer, **A, B** or **C**.

1   You hear two people discussing a play.
    Who is going to see it?

    A   the man

    B   both of them

    C   neither of them

            1

2   You will hear an announcement about a television programme.
    What is the programme about?

    A   Indian religion

    B   Indian cooking

    C   Indian history

            2

3   Listen to this man speaking.
    Who is he?

    A   a traffic policeman

    B   a taxi driver

    C   a tour guide

            3

4   In a hotel, the receptionist is giving a guest his bill.
    What is the problem?

    A   The man has made a mistake.

    B   It is someone else's bill.

    C   There is a mistake in the bill.

            4

5   You hear someone talking on a public phone.
Who is he talking to?

    A   a friend

    B   a repair man

    C   a taxi company

                                                          5

6   In a museum café you overhear two people talking.
What did the woman feel about the exhibition?

    A   She was impressed.

    B   She was disappointed.

    C   She was bored.

                                                          6

7   You hear a woman telephoning a furniture store.
What does she want the store to do?

    A   deliver her table on Tuesday

    B   leave the table at her neighbour's house

    C   confirm the delivery time

                                                          7

8   You hear two people in a travel agent's arguing about a trip.
What do they disagree about?

    A   whether to go or not

    B   how much it will cost

    C   when to go

                                                          8

Part 2

You will hear part of a local radio programme, in which the presenters give the answers to a quiz. For Questions **9–18**, fill in the answers to the quiz.

Local History Quiz

Alexander Byfleet was [**9**]

The Buy Easy Supermarket is where [**10**] used to be.

Jimmy Milburn was [**11**]

The boot factory in Dean Road is now [**12**]

A hundred years ago,
the town's main industry was [**13**]

The oldest building in the town is [**14**]

The novel by Anthony Diprose
that was set in the town is called [**15**]

In 1976 there was [**16**] in Wood Lane.

The building that opened in 1985 is [**17**]

This year [**18**] is one hundred years old.

Part 3

You will hear five people talking on the radio about their jobs. For Questions **19–23**,
choose from the list **A–F** how each got his or her job originally. Use the letters only
once. There is one extra letter which you do not need to use.

A   The person hadn't planned to change jobs.

Speaker 1 [ ] **19**

B   No one else came to the interview.

Speaker 2 [ ] **20**

C   Someone else refused the job.

Speaker 3 [ ] **21**

D   This person refused the job first.

Speaker 4 [ ] **22**

E   This person needed help to get to the interview.

Speaker 5 [ ] **23**

F   This person got the job because of a mistake.

Part 4

You will hear a young actress being interviewed on the radio. Answer Questions **24–30**, by writing **T** for **TRUE** or **F** for **FALSE** in the boxes provided.

---

24 Beatrice wanted to play the piano when she was young.

	24

25 She wanted to train as a circus performer when she was seven.

	25

26 She performed in front of large audiences at an early age.

	26

27 Elizabeth was a school friend.

	27

28 Beatrice appreciated Elizabeth's opinion of her acting.

	28

29 Beatrice has a good memory.

	29

30 She goes to dance classes to improve her dancing.

	30

PAPER 5   SPEAKING (approximately 14 minutes)

You take the Speaking test with another candidate, referred to here as your partner. There are two examiners. One will speak to you and your partner and the other will just be listening. Both examiners will award marks.

Part 1 (3 minutes)
The examiner asks you and your partner questions about yourselves. You may be asked about things like 'your home town', 'your interests', 'your career plans', etc.

Part 2 (4 minutes)
The examiner gives you two photographs and asks you to talk about them for about one minute. The examiner then asks your partner a question about your photographs and your partner responds briefly.

Then the examiner gives your partner two different photographs. Your partner talks about these photographs for about one minute. This time the examiner asks you a question about your partner's photographs and you respond briefly.

Part 3 (3 minutes)
The examiner asks you and your partner to talk together. You may be asked to discuss something, solve a problem or perhaps come to a decision about something. For example, you might be asked to decide the best way to use some rooms in a language school. The examiner gives you a picture to help you but does not join in the conversation.

Part 4 (4 minutes)
The examiner asks some further questions, which lead to a more general discussion of what you have talked about in Part 3.

Test 3

PAPER 1 READING (1 hour 15 minutes)

Part 1

You are going to read an article about ice skating. Choose the most suitable heading from the list **A–I** for each part (**1–7**) of the article. There is one extra heading which you do not need to use. There is an example at the beginning (**0**).

Mark your answers **on the separate answer sheet**.

A	Preparing yourself
B	The benefits of the sport
C	When things go wrong
D	Different skating techniques
E	A change in approach
F	The right attitude
G	Moving off
H	Holding your body correctly
I	How it all started

ICE SKATING

0	I

Ice skating has a history of thousands of years. Archaeologists have discovered skates made from animal bone. It seems that bone skates were used until the introduction of iron into Scandinavia about the year 200 AD. Among the Scandinavian upper classes, skating was seen as an essential skill.

1

In the early twentieth century, skating was stylish and reserved, but at the 1924 Winter Olympics, 11-year-old Sonja Henie introduced a more athletic attitude which inspired a new wave of popularity. Nowadays art and athletics are combined and modern skating is both graceful and physically demanding.

2

For the beginner, balance and control are all important and speed can only increase with proficiency. The position of your body plays a great part in balance. Legs slightly bowed and the knees bent keep the body weight centred; in effect the body leans slightly forward in this position. For skating, probably more than any other sport or recreation, relaxation is vital.

3

For the starting position, the heels should almost be touching and the feet should be turned outwards. While pushing forward with the back foot, you make a very small movement with the other foot. Fairly easy, isn't it? If you can keep this up for a while, you can then slowly increase the length of your movements as you gain experience.

4

Knowing how to fall must be learnt among the skater's first skills. Even the best of the professionals fall. In order to fall without injury, you should be as relaxed as possible. In this way the shock of hitting the ice is lessened. To get up, use your hands to get into a kneeling position, then stand.

5

Once you have learnt to move on the ice with confidence, there are various styles to be practised – figure skating, free style, distance, speed, skating in pairs, and so on – but the basis of them all, and by far the best approach, is first to learn figure skating and then elementary freestyle. With proper guidance available at most of the ice rinks throughout the country, the basic figures can soon be learnt and the turns, jumps and spins of elementary free style will soon follow.

6

If you look at any good or professional skater, you will see how relaxed they are and how easily they move. To achieve this an exercise programme should be regularly practised. It can be dangerous to skate with a stiff body and warm-up exercises should at least include those for the legs, back and shoulders, with special emphasis on the ankles and the knees. After a long or intense session, the same exercises should be used afterwards to avoid stiffness.

7

Skating improves balance, co-ordination, relaxation and movement. It improves heart and lung activity and generally strengthens the body. Combined with swimming or jogging, it provides a great programme for all-round health and fitness.

You are going to read a newspaper article about a triathlete. The triathlon is a sport consisting of running, swimming and cycling. For Questions **8–15**, choose the answer **A, B, C** or **D** which you think fits best according to the text.

Mark your answers **on the separate answer sheet**.

Why would a schoolgirl want to swim 1500m, cycle 40km and then run 10km? Because 'it's fun'.

Teenager with a taste for endurance

WANTED: Sports-mad training partner for triathlete, preferably female. Chance to work with potential Olympic champion. Should be extremely keen on distance running (regular 15km sessions), distance swimming (addiction to winter training in cold rivers useful) and distance cycling (love of 100km an advantage). Ability to do all three without a rest essential.

The triathlon promises to be one of the most popular Olympic sports. Recently it has drawn huge crowds fascinated (and horrified) by athletes swimming 1500m, cycling 40km, then running 10km without stopping. Great for those watching, maybe, but what makes the triathletes want to punish their bodies so much? And what makes an attractive 17-year-old, with excellent academic results, give up everything for the doubtful pleasures it offers?

Melanie Sears has not yet learnt those often-repeated phrases about personal satisfaction, mental challenge and higher targets that most athletes automatically use when asked similar questions. 'You swim for 1500m, then run out of the water and jump on your bike, still wet. Of course, then you freeze. When the 40km cycle ride is over, you have to run 10km, which is a long way when you're feeling exhausted. But it's great fun, and all worth it in the end,' she says.

Melanie entered her first triathlon at 14. 'I won the junior section – but then I was the only junior taking part. It seemed so easy that I was waving at my team-mates as I went round.' Full of confidence, she entered the National Championships, and although she had the second fastest swim and the fastest run, she came nowhere. 'I was following this man and suddenly we came to the sea. We realised

then that we had gone wrong. I ended up cycling 20 kilometres too far. I cried all the way through the running.'

But she did not give up and is determined that she never will. 'Sometimes I wish I could stop, because then the pain would be over, but I am afraid that if I let myself stop just once, I would be
35 tempted to do it again.' Such doggedness draws admiration from Steve Trew, the sport's director of coaching. 'I've just been testing her fitness,' he says, 'and she worked so hard on the running machine that it finally threw her off and into a wall. She had given it everything, but whereas most people step off when they realise they can't go any further, she just kept on.'

Melanie was top junior in this year's European Triathlon Championships, finishing 13th. 'I was almost as good as the top three in swimming and running, but much slower at cycling. That's why I'm working very hard at it.' She is trying to talk her long-suffering parents, who will carry the £1,300 cost of her trip to New Zealand for this year's World Championships, into buying a £2,000 bike ('It's a special deal, with £1,000 off') so she can try national 25 km and 100 km races later this year.

But there is another price to pay. Her punishing training sessions have made her a bit of a recluse. 'I don't have a social life,' she says. 'I'm not a party animal anyway. After two hours' hard swimming on Friday nights, I just want to go to sleep. But I phone and write to the other girls in the team.' What does she talk about? Boys? Clothes? 'No, what sort of times they are achieving.'

Where will all this single-mindedness end? Melanie has tried other events. She has had a go at the triathlon 'sprint', for example, where you only have to swim 750m, cycle 20km and run 5km. She wants to enter even tougher events than the triathlon. 'The big trouble is, I have no one of my age to train with,' she says. Funny, that.

8 What is the purpose of the 'advertisement' in the first paragraph?
   A to encourage people to take up the triathlon
   B to explain why the triathlon is becoming more popular
   C to describe how difficult the triathlon is
   D to criticise people who do the triathlon

9 How does Melanie differ from other athletes, according to the writer?
   A Her personality is not like theirs.
   B Her aims are different from theirs.
   C She worries less than they do.
   D She expresses herself differently.

10 What upset Melanie during the National Championships?
   A She was tricked by another competitor.
   B She realised she couldn't cycle as fast as she thought.
   C She felt that she had let her team-mates down.
   D She made a mistake during part of the race.

11 What is meant by Melanie's 'doggedness' in line 35?
   A She continues despite all difficulties.
   B She feels less pain than most people.
   C She knows her own limits.
   D She likes to please her coach.

12 What is Melanie trying to persuade her parents to do?
   A let her compete in longer races
   B buy a special bike for her
   C pay for her to go to New Zealand
   D give her half the cost of a bike

13 What does Melanie say about her relationships with her team-mates?
   A She only discusses the triathlon with them.
   B She would like to see them more often.
   C She dislikes discussing boys or clothes with them.
   D She thinks they find her way of life strange.

14 What does the writer mean by the phrase 'Funny, that' at the end of the article?
   A It is strange that more young people do not take up the triathlon.
   B It is clear that Melanie enjoys training for tough events.
   C It is amusing to hear people's reactions to the triathlon.
   D It is understandable that Melanie does not have a training partner of her own age.

15 What is the writer's attitude to Melanie?
   A He is worried that her social life is interfering with her sport.
   B He believes that success has come to her too young.
   C He thinks that she is an extraordinary teenager.
   D He envies her enormous determination to succeed.

Part 3

You are going to read a travel article about Malaysia. Seven paragraphs have been removed from the article. Choose from the paragraphs **A–H** the one which fits each gap (**16–21**). There is one extra paragraph which you do not need to use. There is an example at the beginning (**0**).

Mark your answers **on the separate answer sheet**.

Visit to Malaysia

Paul Forster goes to a kite-flying festival, and spends a nervous night in the forest.

Adnan Ali smiled broadly as I presented him with his torn kite. 'You have to keep it,' he said, 'it's traditional – if the line breaks, finders are keepers ... and anyway, I've plenty more.' He indicated a pile of intricately decorated kites at his feet. All were precisely 120cm wide and long, and made of tissue paper and split bamboo.

0	**H**

In the centre of the beach stood 10 platforms, where helpers held up the kites, and a row of tense competitors holding the lines of their kites waited for the countdown. On the blast of the whistle, the crowd roared and the kites rose into the air like rockets.

16	

'Flying kites isn't so difficult,' said Adnan, 'but making them takes real skill. Visit me at home and I'll show you how it's done.' The invitation was one of five I'd received that day, and I decided to accept.

17	

Instead I explored the southern half of the state, pointing my car inland on the road to Kuala Lumpur, into granite mountains dripping with luxuriant rainforest. I took a wrong turning and the smooth road ended suddenly at a river.

18	

Before setting off, it would have been useful to know that nearly all of this distance was uphill, steep and slippery. When I got to the track, however, I found a chap waiting with a flask of tea.

⟫→

19

Night was totally black, full of different sounds. A waterfall roared nearby and thousands of living things moved and squeaked. In the morning there was a tremendous view over five ranges of green mountains. In the afternoon it rained.

20

Other thoughts included the possibility of my car being swept away (it sometimes happens)

and the likelihood of drowning if I opened my mouth. Fortunately the car was still there, covered in mud, at the bottom of the track.

21

But in the asking there was nothing but friendliness. Kelantan might be best known for its kites but I remember it more for its human kindness.

A   First wind, then lightning lashed the treetops. Seconds later I was wet through. Sliding downhill, I wondered how the scores of giant butterflies avoided the enormous drops.

B   A needle-shaped boat was waiting to ferry pedestrians across. Near it, a small sign caught my eye. It pointed up a footpath into the forest and read: 'Jelawang Jungle 3 km.'

C   No one is a stranger for long here. Back in Kota Bahru, Kelantan's capital, everyone fired questions at me: 'Where are you from?' 'How old are you?'

D   Then he led off down the sandy track, pointing to the trees on either side: guava, papaya, two types of mango, banana and a green fruit containing cashew nuts. 'With fish from the sea and rice, we have everything here,' he said.

E   Back in his house I drank cold milky tea and ate fish crackers in a large polished room. As dusk fell, he told me to come again the next day to start rebuilding his kite but my plans didn't allow it.

F   This was Baha, who looked after a tented kitchen and a dozen or so bamboo huts. I decided to stay there, determined not to think twice about insects crawling under my thin foam mattress.

G   More than 500 men and boys had registered for the competition, which runs for five days every year. Each had entered four different designs which were to be judged on decoration, stability in the air and flying efficiency.

H   We sat down next to them in the shade of the whispering coniferous trees that are behind the Beach of the Seven Lagoons in the state of Kelantan, and looked out over Malaysia's biggest and most serious kite festival.

Part 4

You are going to read a magazine article in which people are interviewed about shopping. For Questions **22–35**, choose from the people (**A–I**). The people may be chosen more than once. When more than one answer is required, these may be given in any order. There is an example at the beginning (**0**).

Mark your answers **on the separate answer sheet**.

Which of the people A–I

lets another person take care of some of the shopping?	**0**	**B**
compares prices before buying things?	**22**	
finds it impossible to resist buying things?	**23**	
sometimes doesn't admit how much she has spent?	**24**	
prefers spending her time on activities other than shopping?	**25**	
feels unhappy when she cannot afford to go shopping?	**26**	
does not need to buy clothes very often?	**27**	
prefers going to the shops at quiet times?	**28**	
is critical of the way shops are run?	**29**	
accepts that her way of shopping is risky?	**30**	**31**
goes shopping when she is unhappy?	**32**	
sometimes buys things she had not planned to buy?	**33**	
enjoys shopping with other people?	**34**	**35**

What sort of shopper are you?

Love it or hate it, we all go shopping. But there are different types of shopper. Do you know which kind you are? Abby Edwards asked around . . .

A   Melanie, 22, dancer

I'm an addict – I can't spend enough money! When I have the cash I'm out there and then I don't get miserable. I definitely have difficulty walking past sale signs. My boyfriend's exactly the same, so we often drag each other around the shops. We're an addicted couple!

B   Brenda, 40, office manager

I'm a reluctant shopper. My husband does most of the food shopping because he does the cooking and knows what he likes. I don't spend much time shopping for clothes ... I do take my 6-year-old son and 14-year-old daughter out to get clothes, but I don't enjoy that either, as we all have different tastes. I don't spend money on myself regularly, so when I do splash out I tend to feel guilty and rarely tell my husband how much I've spent – I always knock the price down a bit! The real price always sounds so shocking.

C   Juliet, 28, personnel manager

I only shop for essentials – I hate shopping and only go when I really have to. When I do, I know what I want and I won't settle for anything else. I find shopping tiring and there's always something I'd rather be doing.

D   Anita, 35, TV producer

I like a good look round every now and then but I tend to know what I want, and where to find it. I don't waste time and I get in and out as quickly as I can. I do have hidden mistakes at the back of my wardrobe though – so maybe I'm a careful shopper who sometimes gets particular purchases wrong!

E   Lizzie, 41, secretary

I don't enjoy shopping in the least. I really dislike shopping for clothes as I can never find what I want, or anyone to help me look for it. The shops are too noisy, everything is disordered and I find it an absolute nightmare. Fortunately, I rarely have to shop for clothes as most of my clothes are given to me. As for food shopping, I go to the local supermarket once a week and get it over and done with quickly!

F   Lisa, 22, actress

I'm probably a happy shopper. Sometimes I'll go out for a look around the shops with my girlfriends – and we'll often end up spending. I don't usually go out with a certain item in mind, but if something catches my eye I'll buy it.

≫→

G | Suki, 26, art gallery assistant

I'm a careful shopper – I like going, but I don't really buy very much. I usually know what I want and I seldom go crazy. I do sometimes shop to cheer myself up – but I usually end up feeling much worse because I've spent too much!

H | Ann-Marie, 29, nursery worker

I love shopping – but only on certain days and never on a Saturday, as it's far too busy. I'd say I'm a careful shopper ... I always set off with a fair idea of what I want, and I never snap things up immediately. I have to look in other shops, in case I can find a better bargain – I take ages!

I | Linda, 32, restaurant manager

I'm an unwilling shopper – maybe because I work in the city centre, the shops have lost their attraction for me. When I have to, I'll drag myself out – but I don't bother to try things on, it's far too much trouble. Clothes I buy don't always fit, but I don't mind too much and I'd rather make a few mistakes than have to go into shops and make a lot of effort!

PAPER 2   WRITING (1 hour 30 minutes)

Part 1

You **must** answer this question.

1 You recently entered a competition for learners of English. You have just received this letter from the organisers of the competition, on which you have written some notes.

Congratulations! We are very pleased to inform you that you have won first prize in our competition: a FREE week for yourself and a friend in Los Angeles or New York.

someone to meet us at the airport?

This includes:

*   Free return flights

*   Accommodation for you both in a 3-star central hotel — *which hotel?*

*   Three meals a day

*   Spending allowance —— *???*

*   A guide (if you want) — *yes, please*

We now need to know which city you would both like to go to, your preferred travel dates, and any special arrangements you would like us to make for you. — *Yes!*

We look forward to hearing from you and we will then send you the tickets.

Yours sincerely

Caroline Riley

Competition Organiser

Read the letter carefully. Then write a reply giving the information requested and also covering the notes you have written on the letter.
Write a **letter** of between **120** and **180** words in an appropriate style on the next page. Do not write any addresses.

Question 1

....

....

....

....

....

....

....

....

....

....

....

....

....

....

....

....

....

....

....

....

....

....

....

....

....

....

....

....

....

Visual materials for Paper 5

1A

1B

2A

2B

1C

1D

2C

2D

1E

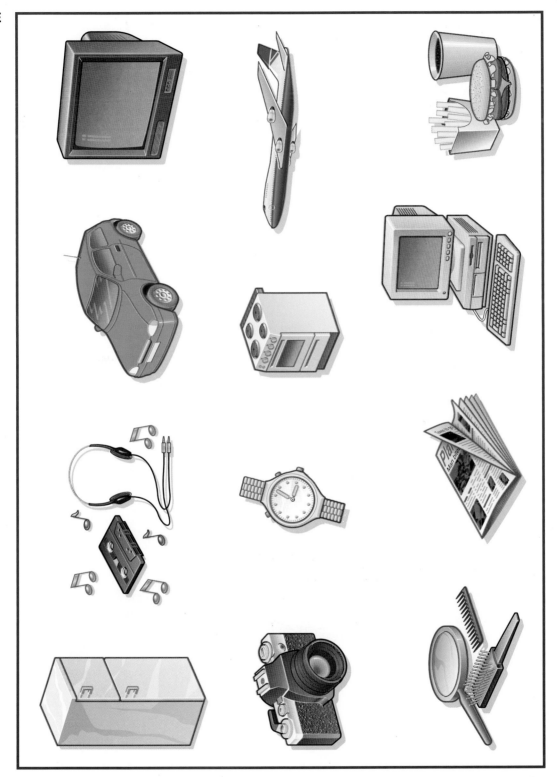

2E

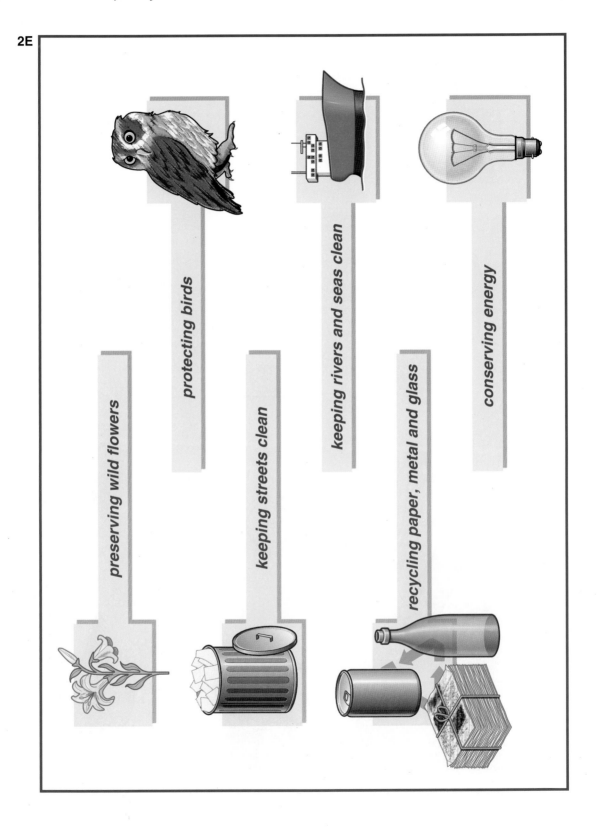

protecting birds

keeping rivers and seas clean

conserving energy

preserving wild flowers

keeping streets clean

recycling paper, metal and glass

3A

3B

4A

4B

3C

3D

4C

4D

3E

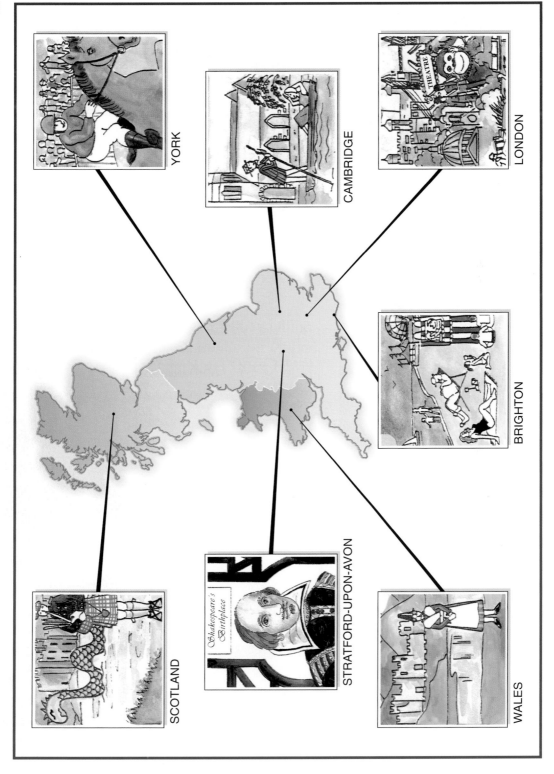

4E

© Liz Dakin 1997.

© Emma Davis 1994.

© Hardcorn 94. Made in the UK.

© Hallmark Cards, UK.

© Hallmark Cards, inc.

© Hallmark Cards, inc.

© Hallmark Cards, inc.

© Hallmark Cards UK.

Part 2

Write an answer to **one** of the Questions **2–5** in this part. Write your answer in **120–180** words in an appropriate style on the next page. Put the question number in the box.

2   Your English pen-friend wants to start learning your language and has written to you for advice and information. Write a letter to your pen-friend, giving advice about how to learn your language **and** telling him or her what you think the main difficulties will be. Do not write any addresses.

   Write your **letter**.

3   Your teacher has asked you to write a story for the school's English language magazine. It must begin with the following words:

   I wanted to do my best; I didn't want to lose. Now, finally, it was time to play.

   Write your **story.**

4   You have a part-time job in a bookshop. The manager wants to make the shop more popular with young people and has asked you to write a report making some recommendations.

   Write a **report** for your manager.

5   Answer **one** of the following two questions based on your reading of **one** of these set books.

   Great Expectations – Charles Dickens   *Brave New World* – Aldous Huxley
   Rebecca – Daphne du Maurier   *Pygmalion* – G. B. Shaw
   Crime Never Pays – Oxford Bookworm Collection

   Your answer should contain enough detail to make it clear to someone who may not have read the book. Write **(a)** or **(b)** as well as the number **5** in the question box, and the **title** of the book next to the box.

   Either   **(a)**   You and your colleagues would like to use the college video equipment to film one part of the book which you have read. Write a **composition**, describing the scene you would choose to film. Give your reasons.

   Or   **(b)**   Do you think that reading books in English can help students to study the English language? Write a **composition**, explaining your view with reference to the book which you have read.

Question	

PAPER 3   USE OF ENGLISH (1 hour 15 minutes)

Part 1

For Questions **1–15**, read the text below and decide which answer **A, B, C** or **D** best
fits each space. There is an example at the beginning **(0)**.
Mark your answers **on the separate answer sheet**.

Example:

0 A territory   **B** scenery   **C** setting   **D** land

0	A	B	C	D

AN ITALIAN VILLAGE IN WALES

The **(0)** ..... in North Wales is magnificent and so this area is very popular with
tourists. Situated on a dramatic part of the rocky coastline is a village, **(1)** ..... in
Britain, called Portmeirion. The dream of the architect Clough Williams-Ellis, its
construction began in 1925 and he finally **(2)** ..... in finishing the **(3)** ..... in 1973.
The result is a copy of a small, and very beautiful, Italian village.

As you wander down the **(4)** ..... paths towards the village you can **(5)** ..... the
sea through the trees, and there is a marvellous **(6)** ..... of the whole coastline
from the top of the church tower. **(7)** ..... the houses, shops and restaurants,
there is a luxury hotel, which seems, at **(8)** ..... tide, almost to float on the water.

Most of the houses are **(9)** ..... to visitors in the summer months, **(10)** ..... a few
people do live in Portmeirion all year **(11)** ..... . It is possible for **(12)** ..... to visit
the village for the day **(13)** ..... payment of a small entrance **(14)** .... Late
spring and early autumn are the best times to visit, **(15)** ..... in the early morning
when the only sound that can be heard is the splashing of the water in the
fountains.

1 **A** single   **B** unique   **C** particular   **D** only

2 **A** succeeded   **B** managed   **C** resulted   **D** achieved

3 **A** task   **B** attempt   **C** effort   **D** labour

4 **A** curling   **B** winding   **C** rolling   **D** waving

5 **A** glimpse   **B** glance   **C** look   **D** catch

6 **A** display   **B** view   **C** sight   **D** outlook

7 **A** As well   **B** More than   **C** In addition to   **D** Apart

8 **A** complete   **B** big   **C** maximum   **D** high

9 **A** charged   **B** paid   **C** let   **D** borrowed

10 **A** although   **B** otherwise   **C** even   **D** despite

11 **A** by   **B** along   **C** round   **D** down

12 **A** spectators   **B** onlookers   **C** observers   **D** sightseers

13 **A** in   **B** over   **C** from   **D** on

14 **A** ticket   **B** fee   **C** fare   **D** subscription

15 **A** particularly   **B** exactly   **C** precisely   **D** distinctly

Part 2

For Questions **16–30**, read the text below and think of the word which best fits each space. Use only **one** word in each space. There is an example at the beginning **(0)**. Write your answers **on the separate answer sheet**.

Example: | **0** | in |

THE LONDON UNDERGROUND

In 1863, the first underground passenger railway **(0)** .... the world opened in London. Called the Metropolitan, **(16)** .... ran for just under seven kilometres and allowed people **(17)** .... avoid the terrible crowds on the roads above as **(18)** .... travelled to and from work. It took three years to complete and **(19)** .... built using an interesting method. This involved digging up the road, laying the track and then building **(20)** .... strong roof over the top. When all **(21)** .... had been done, the road surface was replaced.

Steam engines were used to pull the carriages and it must **(22)** .... been fairly unpleasant **(23)** .... the passengers, with all the smoke and noise. However, the railway quickly proved to **(24)** .... a great success and within six months more **(25)** .... 25,000 people were using it every day.

Later, engineers were able to construct railways in a system of deep tunnels, **(26)** .... became known **(27)** .... the Tube. This development was only possible with **(28)** .... introduction of electric-powered engines and lifts. The Central London Railway was **(29)** .... of the most successful of these new lines, and was opened in 1900. It **(30)** .... white-painted tunnels and bright red carriages, and proved extremely popular with the public.

Part 3

For Questions **31–40**, complete the second sentence so that it has a similar meaning to the first sentence, using the word given. **Do not change the word given**. You must use between two and five words, including the word given.

Here is an example **(0)**.

Example:

0 You must do exactly what the manager tells you.

carry

You must .... instructions exactly.

The gap can be filled by the words 'carry out the manager's' so you write:

0	carry out the manager's

Write **only the missing words** on the separate answer sheet.

---

31 I haven't seen my brother since he left for Australia.
last

The .... my brother was before he left for Australia.

32 The price of the holiday includes the cost of insurance.
is

The cost of insurance .... the price of the holiday.

33 'If you wanted to take my car, you should have asked me first,' said Tom to his son.
without

Tom criticised his son for having .... him first.

34 You ought to get your bicycle brakes repaired immediately.
better

You .... your bicycle brakes repaired immediately.

35 Sarah is not usually late.
like

It is .... late.

36 I would prefer it if nobody else knew what happened last night.
want

I don't .... what happened last night.

37 It was snowing so they cancelled the football match.
owing

The football match .... the snow.

38 The taxi may be expensive so take plenty of money.
case

Take plenty of money .... expensive.

39 They couldn't understand the lecturer because she spoke so fast.
too

The lecturer spoke .... understand.

40 The manager said I could have three days off.
permission

The manager .... to have three days off.

Part 4

For Questions **41–55**, read the text below and look carefully at each line. Some of the lines are correct, and some have a word which should not be there.
If a line is correct, put a tick **(✓)** by the number **on the separate answer sheet**. If a line has a word which should **not** be there, write the word **on the separate answer sheet**. There are two examples at the beginning (**0** and **00**).

Examples:

0	✓
00	travel

AN IMPORTANT MESSAGE

0 When you arrive at the airport it is best if you take

00 a taxi travel all the way to my house. It doesn't cost a lot

41 and it is much less trouble than by finding the right train

42 or bus. In any of case, even if you do catch a train or

43 bus, you still have to take a taxi when you will get to

44 the centre of the city. This is because I don't live near a

45 train station or bus stop. When you reach to my house,

46 you must first go the next door and ask for Mrs Evans.

47 She has the key to my house, which you will need it because,

48 as you know, I won't be back until Wednesday, and

49 you will be arriving on Sunday. Mrs Evans has a photo

50 of you to make sure she only gives in the key to the right

51 person. When you go into the house, you will find various

52 useful leaflets and things, including those maps and timetables.

53 There is a quite lot of food in the fridge and in the freezer,

54 which you are welcome to help yourself to. If you need fresh

55 milk or anything else other, Mrs Evans will explain to you how

to get to the nearest shops.

Part 5

For Questions **56–65**, read the text below. Use the word given in capitals at the end of each line to form a word that fits in the space in the same line. There is an example at the beginning **(0)**. Write your answers **on the separate answer sheet**.

Example:

0	closure

GOOD NEWS FOR BRADSTONE

Following the unexpected **(0)** *closure* last year of a number of factories   **CLOSE**

in and around Bradstone, leading to a sharp rise in local **(56)** ..... ,   **EMPLOY**

it is very good to hear that the **(57)** ..... of a new high-technology   **CONSTRUCT**

centre will begin **(58)** ..... on the site of one of the old factories.   **SHORT**

Network UK, the company responsible, made the **(59)** ..... yesterday.   **ANNOUNCE**

They said they would soon start **(60)** ..... for two hundred new staff   **ADVERTISE**

who are suitably **(61)** ..... for the new jobs available. The management   **QUALIFY**

said it was also their **(62)** ..... to offer fifty job-training positions for   **INTEND**

young people who have **(63)** ..... left school. They want to build up a   **RECENT**

dynamic, well-trained and **(64)** ..... team and believe that they can   **ENTHUSIASM**

contribute to making Bradstone a happy and **(65)** ..... town once again.   **WEALTH**

PAPER 4   LISTENING (approximately 40 minutes)

Part 1

You will hear people talking in eight different situations. For Questions **1–8**, choose the best answer, **A, B** or **C**.

---

1   Listen to this girl talking about a book she has just read.
What does she think about the book?

   A   It is inaccurate.

   B   It is depressing.

   C   It is too long.

> 1

2   You hear a woman talking to a man.
What is she doing?

   A   complaining about something

   B   suggesting something

   C   explaining something

> 2

3   You overhear a woman talking about somewhere she visited on holiday.
What is she describing?

   A   a palace

   B   an art gallery

   C   a department store

> 3

4   Listen to this couple talking about a parcel they have received.
Why are they disappointed?

   A   They ordered a different item.

   B   It is not suitable.

   C   It has been damaged.

> 4

5 You hear a local shopkeeper talking about tourists.
What is he complaining about?

  A the way they treat local people

  B the increasing numbers of them

  C how little money they spend

	5

6 You switch on the radio and hear something being read.
What is it?

  A a weather forecast

  B a news report

  C a story

	6

7 You overhear two people talking as they leave their office.
What is the woman going to do this weekend?

  A play tennis

  B go to the beach

  C work in the garden

	7

8 You hear a man talking about his life.
How does he feel?

  A determined

  B hopeful

  C regretful

	8

Part 2

You will hear a magazine editor talking on the radio about a competition. For Questions **9–18**, complete the notes.

Prize: [_____ **9**] worth £500

Number of photographs: [_____ **10**]

Category 1: photos of [_____ **11**]

Category 2: photos of [_____ **12**]

Category 3: photos of [_____ **13**]

Each photo must be accompanied by: [_____ **14**]

and [_____ **15**]

Name of magazine: [_____ **16**]

Judged by: Miranda Smith, the magazine's [_____ **17**]

Results in: [_____ **18**]

Part 3

You will hear five different women talking about the activities they enjoy. For Questions **19–23**, choose from the list **A–F** what each speaker says about her activity. Use the letters only once. There is one extra letter which you do not need to use.

A I have been doing this activity since childhood.

| Speaker 1 | | 19 |

B I prefer to exercise alone.

| Speaker 2 | | 20 |

C I like meeting new people through this activity.

| Speaker 3 | | 21 |

D I enjoy the competition.

| Speaker 4 | | 22 |

E I find this activity relaxing.

| Speaker 5 | | 23 |

F I like the teamwork.

Part 4

You will hear a conversation in which Alan asks his friends Bob and Carol about a sports club. Answer Questions **24–30**, by writing **B** for Bob, **C** for Carol, or **N** for Neither in the boxes provided.

---

24 Who usually chooses the same activity?

24

25 Who has been trying some new equipment?

25

26 Who objects to the rise in membership fees?

26

27 Who enjoys the friendly atmosphere?

27

28 Who is critical of some instructors?

28

29 Who is dissatisfied with some of the facilities?

29

30 Who is disappointed with a recent addition?

30

PAPER 5   SPEAKING (approximately 14 minutes)

You take the Speaking test with another candidate, referred to here as your partner. There are two examiners. One will speak to you and your partner and the other will just be listening. Both examiners will award marks.

Part 1 (3 minutes)
The examiner asks you and your partner questions about yourselves. You may be asked about things like 'your home town', 'your interests', 'your career plans', etc.

Part 2 (4 minutes)
The examiner gives you two photographs and asks you to talk about them for about one minute. The examiner then asks your partner a question about your photographs and your partner responds briefly.

Then the examiner gives your partner two different photographs. Your partner talks about these photographs for about one minute. This time the examiner asks you a question about your partner's photographs and you respond briefly.

Part 3 (3 minutes)
The examiner asks you and your partner to talk together. You may be asked to discuss something, solve a problem or perhaps come to a decision about something. For example, you might be asked to decide the best way to use some rooms in a language school. The examiner gives you a picture to help you but does not join in the conversation.

Part 4 (4 minutes)
The examiner asks some further questions, which lead to a more general discussion of what you have talked about in Part 3.

Test 4

PAPER 1   READING (1 hour 15 minutes)

Part 1

You are going to read a newspaper article about digging for gold. Choose the most suitable heading from the list **A–I** for each part (**1–7**) of the article. There is one extra heading which you do not need to use. There is an example at the beginning (**0**).

Mark your answers **on the separate answer sheet**.

A	The research work
B	Others follow
C	Past success
D	Doubting observers
E	Building the mine
F	Confident of success
G	More funds required
H	Local reaction
I	World-wide search for gold

Father and son start Gold Rush

0	I

Terence and Chris Madden have travelled from Canada's frozen north to the heat of Africa in their search for nature's most desired metals. The father and son team – one an explorer, the other a mineral expert – believe their mine on the side of a Welsh mountain could contain up to 10,000 ounces of gold.

1	

After ten years of digging in the Welsh hills, they are convinced that they are just metres away from a five million dollar vein of gold. 'As we dig, we are finding high levels of gold; now we just need to get a few more metres to where it is concentrated,' said Terence, 68, from Liverpool.

2	

The pair have dedicated their lives to the hunt for gold. Their search began after the father read of pockets of gold worth millions of pounds buried in the 'Dolgellau gold belt', an area around the Welsh town of the same name. While reading 19th century mining journals and newspapers at the Welsh National Library in Aberystwyth, father and son chose the most promising area of land to study.

3	

Since they first cleared away the undergrowth and found bits of gold in the rocks, they have spent the past ten years getting permission for their work from the owners, taking samples of the earth and removing old cars and rubbish. They then set about digging out 150 tonnes of greenstone rock to form a tunnel and a 10-metre shaft.

4	

Now they are running short of money. Having spent their savings chasing their dream, they will have to convince a backer to put £50,000 into the project to lower the mine just a few more metres to where the gold lies. Chris Madden says, 'At the moment, this looks doubtful although we've got quite a few people we can contact.'

5	

As word spread through the valleys last week about the dig, the magic attraction of gold started turning the heads of the inhabitants as well as the gold diggers. Dolgellau relies on tourists, and residents are cautiously hopeful. 'It would encourage more people to come here if they are right,' said Peter Woolven, manager of the Royal Ship Hotel, 'but if these two find gold I hope millions of people are not going to come and hack away at the hillside.'

6	

The Welsh gold industry has gone into steep decline since its height in the late 1880s, when thousands were employed in hundreds of mines dotted around the countryside. One of the last remaining mines at Clogau-St David's, which produced wedding rings for the Queen and the Princess of Wales, closed a month ago.

7	

Now, however, individual gold-diggers are returning. George Hall, another prospector, plans to drive a tunnel deep into the hill on the other side of the ridge from the Maddens. 'Searching for gold is very emotional,' said Hall, 70. 'It's adventurous and exciting, the wonder of uncovering hidden treasure. Maybe I'll be lucky this time.'

Part 2

You are going to read a magazine article about specialist music schools. For Questions **8–15**, choose the answer (**A, B, C** or **D**) which you think fits best according to the text. Mark your answers **on the separate answer sheet**.

SPECIALIST MUSIC SCHOOLS

How to cope with a child who shows outstanding musical ability? It's not always clear how best to develop and encourage their gift. Many parents may even fail to recognise and respond to their child's need until frustration explodes into difficult or uncooperative behaviour. And while most schools are equipped to deal with children who are especially able in academic subjects, the musically gifted require special understanding which may not always be available in an ordinary school – especially one where music is regarded as a secondary activity. Such children – as well as those whose ability is actively encouraged by parents or teachers – may well benefit from the education offered by a specialist music school.

The five music schools in Britain are a relatively recent introduction. They aim to provide a sympathetic environment in which gifted children aged between seven and eighteen can develop their skills to the full under the guidance of professional musicians.

Children at specialist music schools spend between one third and one half of an average day on musical activities, for example, individual lessons (up to three hours a week on first and second instruments), orchestras, chamber groups, voice training, conducting and theory. They also spend several hours a day practising in properly equipped private rooms, sometimes with a teacher. The rest of their time is taken up with a restricted academic programme, which tends to concentrate on the essential subjects – English, maths, basic sciences and languages – although provision can be made for students who wish to study a wider range of subjects. All five British specialist schools are independent, classes are small by normal school standards, with a high teacher/pupil ratio. Most children attending specialist schools tend to be boarders, leaving home to live, eat and sleep full-time at school. This means they spend their formative years in the company of others with similar aims and interests.

What are the disadvantages? An obvious problem is the cost; the fees are high (£12,000– £17,000 a year for boarders). However, each school will make every effort with scholarships and other forms of financial assistance, to help parents of outstandingly gifted children to find the necessary fees. Secondly, not all parents want to send their children to boarding school, specially at a very early age. Almost all the directors of the specialist schools express doubts about the wisdom of admitting children as young as seven into such an intense and disciplined environment. They stress, however, that their main aim is to turn out 'rounded and well-balanced individuals'.

There is little doubt that setting musically gifted children apart from an early age can cause stress. Early signs of musical ability may disappear in teenage years, while natural competitiveness and the pressure to succeed can lead to a crushing sense of failure. But all specialist schools do keep a close watch on the progress of individual pupils, and offer help and advice if needed.

In addition, while most former pupils at music school feel that they benefited enormously from the range of high-quality music teaching available, many express reservations about the wisdom of restricting the academic programme, which definitely takes second place to musical activities. Many musically gifted young people are also highly intelligent, well able to deal with academic pressure, and feel frustrated if their intellectual needs are not met. For these reasons, it may be better to wait until the child is old enough to be able to make his or her own decisions before considering a specialist education.

Those who are equally gifted academically may do very well within a less specialised environment; for instance, at a school with a first class music department, or else by combining a normal school routine with musical training at one of the junior departments at the music colleges. These colleges offer Saturday morning opportunities for individual lessons with fine teachers, plus orchestral and chamber music experience. But this option is clearly not practicable for families living out of reach of London or other major centres.

8   If a child's musical ability is not recognised
    A   the ability may fade away.
    B   the child may misbehave.
    C   the parents may become anxious.
    D   the child may lose interest.

9   What problem may musically gifted children face in ordinary schools?
    A   Music is not seen as an important subject.
    B   Their academic work may suffer.
    C   Schools lack musical equipment.
    D   Parents and teachers do not work together.

10   What makes specialist music schools different from other schools?
    A   The children have mostly one-to-one lessons.
    B   Their working day is longer.
    C   More than half the day is spent on music.
    D   A range of musical training is offered.

11   What do most school directors see as a possible disadvantage for pupils?
    A   They may not be mature enough on arrival.
    B   Poor children may be excluded.
    C   There may be a discipline problem.
    D   They may lose their individuality.

12   A specialist musical education might be stressful for children if
    A   the teachers expect too much of them.
    B   they lose interest in music.
    C   they do not progress as expected.
    D   parents put pressure on them.

13   Past pupils think that they should have
    A   had less academic pressure.
    B   studied more subjects.
    C   worked harder.
    D   concentrated more on music.

14   What would be a good alternative to specialised music schools for gifted children?
    A   having special classes at the weekend
    B   contacting a local orchestra
    C   arranging visits from a specialist music teacher
    D   waiting until they are old enough to go to college

15   Who is this written for?
    A   music teachers
    B   school directors
    C   musically gifted children
    D   parents of musical children

Part 3

You are going to read a magazine article about getting fit. Seven sentences have been removed from the article. Choose from the sentences **A–H** the one which fits each gap (**16–21**). There is one extra sentence which you do not need to use. There is an example at the beginning (**0**).

Mark your answers **on the separate answer sheet**.

GETTING FIT

Exercise is essential for mind, body and spirit. It's one of the best ways to maintain a perfect balance when all around you everything seems more and more unbalanced and the world becomes ever more fast and furious.

| 0 | H |

The reason why there are so many is that it is seriously good for you. There are plenty of reasons why you should exercise and very few – for most of us – why you shouldn't. Exercise improves muscle tone and provides quick changes in body shape. It improves muscle power and promotes good posture – the way in which you hold your body when sitting or standing. It helps prevent those muscle imbalances which can lead to injuries. It provides quick improvement in specific problem areas such as thighs, stomach and upper arms. It improves the condition of the heart and lungs and blood circulation.

Probably all these reasons have been thrown at you time and time again, so maybe you are bored by them and have switched off. | 16 | Did you know that exercise helps to ease depression and tiredness, and that it helps to regulate sleep patterns? Also that exercise is instrumental in controlling stress? Not only this, but exercise can help to relieve certain medical conditions.

By now you should be influenced a little by these arguments. | 17 |

There are plenty of types of exercise you can do – aerobics, calisthenics, jogging, working out with free weights, working on weight machines. There is one point you should note – training too hard and with too much weight may cause injury, so start slowly and carefully. | 18 |

No amount of exercise will improve your body shape if you don't have good posture. | 19 | Not only is a stiff or sagging body unattractive, it also lacks energy and is more likely to suffer from minor health complaints.

If your body tends to slouch, imagine that the top of your head is connected to a helium balloon, which is trying to pull you up into the sky. [20] At the same time, it lengthens the abdomen, making the body look much slimmer. If the chest is well balanced when you are standing, you can see your ankles.

Stretching the muscles improves flexibility and ease of movement, and helps you to maintain correct posture and to prevent muscle tears and injuries caused by overuse. [21] So stretching should play an important part in your exercise routine, which should be performed both slowly and precisely.

The best exercise, therefore, involves a good warm-up, stretching exercises, an energetic workout and definitely a cool down period.

A If not, common sense alone should tell you that exercise is good for you.

B This will help you to lift the chest for fuller and easier breathing.

C All right then, this should make you sit up and take notice.

D This practically determines how you look and feel.

E If done four or five times a week, it will guarantee a more flexible, fitter body.

F If you're not sure, you should consult your doctor on what's good for you personally.

G To help with such physical problems, you need to wake up the circulation by doing any kind of exercise.

H Don't groan because this is yet another article about fitness.

Part 4

You are going to read some information about cookery books. For Questions **22–31**, choose from the books (**A–D**). For Questions **32–35**, choose from the authors (**A–D**). The books and authors may be chosen more than once. There is an example at the beginning (**0**).

Mark your answers **on the separate answer sheet**.

A	**Delia Smith's Complete Cookery Course**
B	**Blanc Mange**
C	**The Cordon Bleu Classic French Cookbook**
D	**The 30-Minute Cook**

Which book . . .

contains recipes from different people?	**0**	**C**
considers mistakes which can be made?	**22**	
includes excellent photographs?	**23**	
has been brought up to date?	**24**	
is concerned with producing food for guests?	**25**	
is organised around the courses of a meal?	**26**	
continues an idea from the author's previous books?	**27**	
marks an important occasion?	**28**	
proves an idea wrong?	**29**	
is based on a very long history of success?	**30**	
would suit both beginners and more experienced cooks?	**31**	

> A   **Delia Smith**
> B   **Raymond Blanc**
> C   **Cordon Bleu Cookery Schools**
> D   **Nigel Slater**

Which author . . .

takes a scientific approach to cooking?   **32** [ ]

has changed recipes for health reasons?   **33** [ ]

writes in a lively manner?   **34** [ ]

deals especially with the demands of modern living?   **35** [ ]

FOOD FOR ALL

We proudly present our own hand-picked special selection of the very best cookbook titles now on offer.

A   Ask anyone to think of a famous TV cook and writer, and it's frequently Delia Smith's name that comes to mind. Her recipes come from all over the world – each marked by her enthusiasm for exciting food, plus her straightforward appreciation of what the average cook can do in the average kitchen. The book that established her reputation is *Delia Smith's Complete Cookery Course*, which has now become the kitchen reference book for the modern cook. Along with simple, but expert, guidance on all aspects of basic and more advanced cookery, Delia mixes her advice with hundreds of superb recipes that are anything but boring. Recently revised, it's more than ever the book that answers the question: 'If I could only have one cookbook, which would it be?'

B   It took Raymond Blanc just 15 years to move from amateur, untrained chef to chef/owner of the most famous French restaurant in Britain. Now, to accompany his first TV series, *Blanc Mange*, comes the book of the same name. Raymond wants to teach us all to be better cooks by demonstrating how and why certain ingredients react in certain ways. Good cooking is easy, in his view, when you really understand what's going on in the pan. Over 80 amazing recipes demonstrate exactly what he means. It's a very practical reference book, which is not above explaining why certain dishes can go wrong and introducing some basic food chemistry to clarify the points made. Monsieur Blanc loves to cook to entertain and, as this book proves, he's very, very good at it.

≫→

89

C *Le Cordon Bleu*, three words which make you think of all that is best in classical French cooking. Over the past 100 years, the expert chefs of this most famous cooking school have trained all levels of students to achieve perfection. Now, to celebrate the school's impressive hundredth anniversary, comes this equally impressive new book, *Le Cordon Bleu Classic French Cookbook*, which contains 100 of the school's most respected recipes. Although the recipes in the book are all classics, they're all still remarkably fresh. While *Le Cordon Bleu* has always carried the flag for traditional French cooking, it has also moved away from rich, creamy sauces and altered its approach to cut down on the killer calories. Starting with a chapter on the basics of sound kitchen procedure, the book follows it up with Appetisers and Starters, Main dishes and, finally, Desserts. Throughout, the recipes are illustrated with step-by-step illustrations plus wonderful shots of the finished dishes. Expert chefs from Cordon Bleu schools around the world have each selected a recipe for which they are famous, and shared their secrets with the reader.

D Fast food? Oh yuk! Surely it's accepted wisdom that good food means a long period of suffering in front of the cooker? Well, Nigel Slater, food editor of *The Observer*, doesn't think so as his new book, *The 30-Minute Cook*, will prove. Fast food, as Nigel says, 'is just what the world wants when it comes home tired and hungry and demanding something good to eat at once.' He's always believed it's perfectly possible to create something tasty in the time it takes to deliver a pizza, and he has already written two very successful books to prove it. In this great new book you'll find more enticing recipes, and each hits the table just 30 minutes after the word 'go'. Nigel has written down, in his jolly and enjoyable style, more than 200 recipes from around the world. Just because he likes his food fast, it doesn't mean this bright young writer doesn't appreciate good food. If you don't believe fast food can be great food, try his recipes: they're simply delicious.

PAPER 2   WRITING (1 hour 30 minutes)

Part 1

You **must** answer this question.

1   You and your classmates are going to have a party to celebrate the end of your course and
    you have offered to book a room for this event. You have seen the advertisement below,
    but you need to know more. Using the notes you have made, write to the Brideswell Inn
    giving relevant details **and** asking for further information.

BRIDESWELL INN

Special 2-course lunch
Mon–Fri
Only £4.95

PRIVATE ROOMS ON REQUEST
VARIOUS SIZES

DISCO ALSO AVAILABLE
EVENING MEALS available from only £6.50

for 30 people

What does this include?
(Get examples of meals –
vegetarian?)

Our date	–	Friday, July 21st
Time	–	20.00 – 24.00
Disco	–	own choice of music?
	–	cost?
Drinks	–	need variety

Write a **letter** of between **120** and **180** words in an appropriate style on the next page. Do not
write any addresses.

Question 1

Part 2

Write an answer to **one** of the Questions **2–5** in this part. Write your answer in **120–180** words in an appropriate style on the next page. Put the question number in the box.

2   You see this announcement in an international magazine.

> ### HOLIDAY COMPETITION
>
> Write an article about the most exciting day you have ever spent
> on holiday **abroad**, explaining to our readers why the day was so special.
>
> The best article will win a weekend for two in London.

Write your **article** for the competition.

3   You have been doing a class project on how people live today. Your teacher has asked you to write a composition giving your opinions on the following statement:

Life is much better today than in the past.

Write your **composition**.

4   Your town has been given a large sum of money which is to be spent on **either** a town-centre park **or** a museum. You have been asked to write a report for the town council, describing the benefits to the town of both projects and saying which one you think should be chosen and why.

Write your **report**.

5   Answer **one** of the following two questions based on your reading of **one** of these set books.

Great Expectations – Charles Dickens   *Brave New World* – Aldous Huxley
Rebecca – Daphne du Maurier   *Pygmalion* – G. B. Shaw
Crime Never Pays – Oxford Bookworm Collection

Either   (a)   'Good stories always have happy endings.' Is this true of the book which you have read? Write a **composition**, explaining why or why not.

Or   (b)   Write a **letter** to a friend, encouraging him or her to read the book which you have read. Give several reasons why you think he or she would enjoy it.

Your answer should contain enough detail to make it clear to someone who may not have read the book. Write **(a)** or **(b)** as well as the number **5** in the question box, and the **title** of the book next to the box.

Question	

....

....

....

....

....

....

....

....

....

....

....

....

....

....

....

....

....

....

....

....

....

....

....

....

....

....

....

....

....

....

PAPER 3   USE OF ENGLISH (1 hour 15 minutes)

Part 1

For Questions **1–15**, read the text below and decide which answer **A, B, C** or **D** best fits each space. There is an example at the beginning **(0)**.
Mark your answers **on the separate answer sheet**.

Example:

0 **A** Apart   **B** Except   **C** Besides   **D** Otherwise

0	A	B	C	D

A FAMOUS STORY WRITER

Beatrix Potter was a story writer whose books about animals have been translated into many languages and read by both children and adults. **(0)** ..... being an author, she was also **(1)** ..... as a very successful farmer.

Born in London in 1866, Beatrix was **(2)** ..... for at home by various servants. Every year she **(3)** ..... the days to her annual holiday in the countryside. She would **(4)** ..... to her London home small animals which she **(5)** ..... and drew. As she grew up, she entertained other children with drawings and stories about these animals. In 1901, she printed a book at her own **(6)** ..... called 'The Tale of Peter Rabbit'. So many **(7)** ..... were sold that she bought a farm, where over the next eight years she wrote many other stories. They all sold very well and readers liked their **(8)** ..... colour drawings.

With her growing **(9)** ..... , Beatrix started buying more farmland, animals and property. After her marriage, at the age of 47, Beatrix stopped writing, **(10)** ..... that she had run out of **(11)** ..... . She became a farmer and **(12)** ..... the rest of her life working with her sheep and awarding prizes at sheep fairs where people often asked for her **(13)** ..... on farming methods.

Today, you can visit her house and **(14)** ..... see the originals of her books and paintings **(15)** ..... in a special gallery.

1   **A**   thought   **B**   regarded   **C**   believed   **D**   judged

2   **A**   attended   **B**   looked   **C**   cared   **D**   minded

3   **A**   counted   **B**   numbered   **C**   imagined   **D**   considered

4   **A**   keep   **B**   get   **C**   give   **D**   take

5   **A**   noticed   **B**   saw   **C**   observed   **D**   remarked

6   **A**   charge   **B**   expense   **C**   earning   **D**   spending

7   **A**   images   **B**   prints   **C**   pages   **D**   copies

8   **A**   complete   **B**   thorough   **C**   particular   **D**   detailed

9   **A**   income   **B**   wages   **C**   pay   **D**   receipt

10   **A**   telling   **B**   speaking   **C**   saying   **D**   talking

11   **A**   views   **B**   ideas   **C**   opinions   **D**   beliefs

12   **A**   involved   **B**   continued   **C**   took   **D**   spent

13   **A**   advice   **B**   mind   **C**   suggestion   **D**   statement

14   **A**   just   **B**   even   **C**   yet   **D**   already

15   **A**   opened   **B**   revealed   **C**   displayed   **D**   demonstrated

Part 2

For Questions **16–30**, read the text below and think of the word which best fits each space. Use only **one** word in each space. There is an example at the beginning **(0)**. Write your answers **on the separate answer sheet**.

Example:

0	a

THE IMPORTANCE OF COMPUTERS

Many of the things we do, depend on receiving information from other people. Catching a train, making **(0)** .... phone call and going to the cinema all involve information **(16)** .... is stored, processed and communicated. In the past this information used to **(17)** .... kept on paper in **(18)** .... form of, for example, books, newspapers and timetables. Now more and more information is put on computers.

Computers play a **(19)** .... in our everyday lives, sometimes **(20)** .... us even realising it. Consider the use **(21)** .... computers in both shops and offices. Big shops, especially chain stores with branches **(22)** .... over the country, have to deal with very large amounts of information. They have to make **(23)** .... there are enough goods on the shelves for customers to buy, they need to be able to re-order before stocks **(24)** .... out, to decide which things are selling well and **(25)** .... on. All these processes **(26)** .... performed quickly and efficiently by computers.

A **(27)** .... of office work in the past involved information on paper. Once it had been dealt **(28)** .... by people, the paper was put **(29)** .... for future reference. This way of working was **(30)** .... particularly easy or fast. A computerised system is much more efficient.

Part 3

For Questions **31–40**, complete the second sentence so that it has a similar meaning to the first sentence, using the word given. **Do not change the word given**. You must use between two and five words, including the word given.

Here is an example **(0)**.

Example:

0 You must do exactly what the manager tells you.

  carry

  You must .... instructions exactly.

  The gap can be filled by the words 'carry out the manager's' so you write:

0	*carry out the manager's*

Write **only the missing words** on the separate answer sheet.

---

31 I didn't know it was your birthday, so I didn't send you a card.
  sent

  If I'd known it was your birthday, I .... you a card.

32 After the match Lucy was so tired that she couldn't eat much.
  too

  After the match Lucy was .... much.

33 I've had enough of your untidiness.
  put

  I refuse .... your untidiness any more.

34 Could I borrow your surfboard please?
  lending

  Would .... your surfboard?

35 My parents didn't let me stay out late when I was younger.
  allowed

  I .... out late when I was younger.

36 How long was your flight from Frankfurt to Seoul?
take

How long .... fly from Frankfurt to Seoul?

37 The last time I went skiing was ten years ago.
for

I .... ten years.

38 Derek has gone to Florida, in spite of being unable to afford such an expensive holiday.
although

Derek has gone to Florida, ... to afford such an expensive holiday.

39 Teenagers aren't buying as many pop records these days.
bought

Not so many pop records .... these days.

40 I regret inviting Nancy to the party.
wish

I .... Nancy to the party.

Part 4

For Questions **41–55**, read the text below and look carefully at each line. Some of the lines are correct, and some have a word which should not be there.
If a line is correct, put a tick **(✓)** by the number **on the separate answer sheet**. If a line has a word which should **not** be there, write the word **on the separate answer sheet**. There are two examples at the beginning (**0** and **00**).

Examples:

0	had
00	✓

A LATE NIGHT

0	Thank you for the book which you had sent me for my
00	birthday last week. I am certain I will really enjoy reading it
41	as the book is one I have been intending to buy it ever since
42	it was being published about two and a half years ago.
43	On Thursday, instead of buying for me a present, my sister
44	took me out for a meal in a restaurant which had been highly
45	recommended her in a local newspaper. The restaurant, which
46	had been open for only two months, was at about 25 kilometres
47	away and we went to there in my sister's car. The meal was
48	excellent and we thoroughly enjoyed ourselves the evening.
49	Unfortunately, after we left the restaurant, we had a problem with
50	the car as that it would not start. We could not find out what the
51	trouble was and decided to leave it behind in the car park
52	until the following day. We asked of a waiter to call a taxi
53	but had to wait over an hour for it to arrive, and so we
54	did not get back our home until very late. I certainly did
55	not feel at all like getting up and going to the work next morning.

Part 5

For Questions **56–65**, read the text below. Use the word given in capitals at the end of each line to form a word that fits in the space in the same line. There is an example at the beginning **(0)**. Write your answers **on the separate answer sheet**.

Example:

0	*suggestion*

HOW TO SUCCEED

Let me make a **(0)** *suggestion* to help you deal with difficult situations.	**SUGGEST**
If, for example, you are taking part in a sports **(56)** ..... ,	**COMPETE**
meeting someone important, or giving a **(57)** ..... in front of a	**PERFORM**
large audience, you will probably be quite **(58)** ..... , and worry	**NERVE**
that you will not be as **(59)** ..... as you would like to be.	**SUCCEED**
What you need to do is to prepare yourself **(60)**	**THOROUGH**
by running through the whole **(61)** ..... over and over again	**ACTIVE**
in your mind, **(62)** ..... going through every detail.	**CARE**
For example, a famous pianist, **(63)** ..... for seven years for	**PRISON**
(64) ..... reasons, could still play magnificently on his release.	**POLITICS**
When asked how he managed to play so well, his **(65)** ..... was	**EXPLAIN**
that he had practised every day in his mind.	

PAPER 4 LISTENING (approximately 40 minutes)

Part 1

You will hear people talking in eight different situations. For Questions **1–8**, choose the best answer, **A, B** or **C**.

---

1 Listen to these people talking about an event.
What event are they talking about?

   A a concert

   B a play

   C a film

                                            1

2 You hear someone talking about a party he has been invited to.
How does he feel about the party?

   A He is nervous about it.

   B He thinks it will be boring.

   C He is unsure what to expect.

                                            2

3 You hear this radio announcement about driving conditions.
What is the main danger tonight?

   A ice

   B snow

   C floods

                                            3

4 You hear part of a radio play.
Where is the scene taking place?

   A on a beach

   B in a hotel

   C in a restaurant

                                            4

5 Listen to this woman telling a friend about a television series.
What is her opinion of it?

    A It is highly original.

    B It is very well-acted.

    C It is the best series on TV.

               5

6 You hear someone talking about a hotel.
Who is the speaker?

    A a hotel receptionist

    B a hotel manager

    C a hotel chef

               6

7 You hear a British actress, Melina Morton, talking on the radio.
Why does Melina live in the USA?

    A Her friends are there.

    B It's good for her job.

    C To be with her husband.

               7

8 You hear someone talking in a tourist information centre.
What is the situation?

    A She has just arrived in the town.

    B She can't find her hotel.

    C She has no place to stay.

               8

Part 2

You will hear part of a radio interview with Mikko Korhonen, a Finnish ice hockey star. For Questions **9–18**, complete the sentences which summarise what the ice hockey star says.

Mikko has wanted to play in
the National League from the age of | **9**

He won a bronze medal in the | **10**

He thinks | **11** | is the best place to play ice hockey.

He didn't play for the first team until | **12**

Because of an argument, there were no games for | **13**

During this period, he decided to | **14**

The team's | **15** | will take place in early April.

The team have not been | **16** | for 10 years.

Mikko is worried he might lose his | **17**

At the end of the season, he will definitely have | **18**

Part 3

You will hear five people talking about their jobs. For Questions **19–23**, choose which of the opinions **A–F** each speaker expresses. Use the letters only once. There is one extra letter which you do not need to use.

A   I like the variety in my work.

Speaker 1	19

B   I find the hours perfect for me.

Speaker 2	20

C   I enjoy the freedom I am given.

Speaker 3	21

D   I have a good future there.

Speaker 4	22

E   I like the friendly atmosphere.

Speaker 5	23

F   I am glad the work is easy.

Part 4

You will hear an interview about adventure sports. For Questions **24–30**, choose the best answer **A, B** or **C**.

24 Stan says that the best thing about walking is that you can

    A get fit by doing it.

    B please yourself how you do it.

    C do it on your own.

24

25 Stan's opinion on scrambling is that

    A people doing it may need to be accompanied.

    B it is unsuitable for beginners.

    C it is more exciting than walking.

25

26 What did Stan discover when he went climbing?

    A It was not enjoyable.

    B It was harder than he expected.

    C It can be very frightening.

26

27 What does Stan say about mountain biking?

    A Britain is not the best place for it.

    B It is more expensive in Britain than elsewhere.

    C It is best where there are lots of downhill slopes.

27

28 Stan's advice on scuba diving is that

    A most of the courses for it are good.

    B it is easier than it seems.

    C you should think carefully before trying it.

28

29 What is Stan's view of skydiving?

    A It is surprisingly popular.

    B It is best when done in teams.

    C Only certain types of people like it.

29

30 What does Stan say about canoeing?

    A You can do it in conditions that suit you.

    B It is best at certain times of the year.

    C There are few places in Britain to do it.

30

PAPER 5 SPEAKING (approximately 14 minutes)

You take the Speaking test with another candidate, referred to here as your partner. There are two examiners. One will speak to you and your partner and the other will just be listening. Both examiners will award marks.

Part 1 (3 minutes)
The examiner asks you and your partner questions about yourselves. You may be asked about things like 'your home town', 'your interests', 'your career plans', etc.

Part 2 (4 minutes)
The examiner gives you two photographs and asks you to talk about them for about one minute. The examiner then asks your partner a question about your photographs and your partner responds briefly.

Then the examiner gives your partner two different photographs. Your partner talks about these photographs for about one minute. This time the examiner asks you a question about your partner's photographs and you respond briefly.

Part 3 (3 minutes)
The examiner asks you and your partner to talk together. You may be asked to discuss something, solve a problem or perhaps come to a decision about something. For example, you might be asked to decide the best way to use some rooms in a language school. The examiner gives you a picture to help you but does not join in the conversation.

Part 4 (4 minutes)
The examiner asks some further questions, which lead to a more general discussion of what you have talked about in Part 3.

Test 1 Key

Paper 1 Reading (1 hour 15 minutes)

Part 1
1 D   2 B   3 F   4 H   5 G   6 E   7 A

Part 2
8 C   9 A   10 B   11 D   12 C   13 A   14 C

Part 3
15 D   16 B   17 C   18 A   19 E   20 H   21 G

Part 4
22/23 C/D (*in any order*)   24 F   25 A   26 B   27 E   28 C
29 E   30 F   31 B   32 E   33/34 C/D (*in any order*)   35 C

Paper 2 Writing (1 hour 30 minutes)

Task-specific mark schemes

Question 1
Content
Major points: Letter should clearly state the reason for writing i.e. the writer wants the friend to join the group on holiday. Must cover essential information about the house, price and dates. Letter must mention at least one place of local interest and one thing to do.
Minor points: Any additional information.

Organisation and cohesion
Clear opening to letter. Suitable paragraphing. Appropriate ending.

Appropriacy of register and format
Informal letter.

Range
Language of description. Future tenses. Vocabulary relating to holidays. Some expression of persuasion.

Target reader
Would have a clear idea of the house and holiday and would consider joining the group of friends.

Question 2

Content

Clear indication of the person and why important (NB Could be a relative as long as importance to **country** is explained). Explanation of what kind of influence the person has had.

Range

Language of description and explanation. Tenses should be appropriate i.e. according to whether the person is still alive or deceased.

Organisation and cohesion

Clear linking between the person and the influence, the description and the explanation.

Appropriacy of register and format

Article format i.e. some paragraphing. Neutral/formal register.

Target reader

Would have a clear picture of the person chosen and their influence on the country.

Question 3

Content

Agree, disagree or both. Should be some mention of the writer's experiences.

Range

Language of opinion, explanation, justification. Vocabulary related to education.

Organisation and cohesion

Clear linking between opinions and writer's experience. Some logical development of ideas.

Appropriacy of register and format

Neutral. Composition format. Some paragraphing essential.

Target reader

Would understand the writer's point of view.

Question 4

Content

Report should identify by name/location/type and then describe at least two places to eat and drink in the town. Explanation of their suitability to students from other countries.

Range

Language of description and explanation. Vocabulary relating to food/drink or setting/ambiance or both.

Organisation and cohesion

Information could be presented in two or more paragraphs/sections. The report must establish the link between place and suitability.

Appropriacy of register and format
Register consistent throughout. Could be informal (student connection).
Sub-headings an advantage, but not essential.

Target reader
Would know of at least two suitable places where the students could eat and
drink.

Question 5(a)

Content
Clear reference to three surprising things in the book and why these were
chosen.

Range
Language of description and explanation.

Organisation and cohesion
Linking of description and explanation.

Appropriacy of register and format
Neutral. Composition layout.

Target reader
Would know why the writer has chosen these three things. (NB A thing could be
a person in this context.)

Question 5(b)

Content
Clear reference to the role to be played and why.

Range
Language of description and explanation.

Organisation and cohesion
Linking of description and explanation.

Appropriacy of register and format
Neutral. Composition layout.

Target reader
Would understand why the writer would want to play the chosen role in a film.

Paper 3   Use of English (1 hour 15 minutes)

Part 1
1 A   2 D   3 A   4 B   5 D   6 B   7 B   8 C   9 C
10 D   11 A   12 C   13 D   14 C   15 A

Part 2
16 of   17 which   18 been   19 them/all/these   20 who
21 with   22 where   23 for   24 this/that   25 from   26 or
27 is   28 its   29 so   30 are

Part 3

Award one mark for each correct section.
31 isn't/is not (1) interested in (1)
32 must not (1) be fed (1)
33 was John's first (1) visit to (1)
34 told Anne (1) (that) he would (1)
35 not (1) as many students (1)
36 mistook/took me (1) for (1) OR confused me (1) with (1) OR believed/
     supposed me (1) to be (1)
37 would/'d (1) like to (1)
38 (his) being unable (1) to swim (1)
39 is no/not a (1) chance of (1)
40 if you (1) had not written (1) OR without you(r) (1) writing/having
     written (1)

Part 4

41 had   42 ✓   43 being   44 much   45 ✓   46 the   47 ✓
48 ✓   49 my   50 ✓   51 about   52 all   53 time   54 while
55 ourselves

Part 5

56 observation(s)   57 behaviour   58 association   59 saying
60 surprisingly   61 unlikely   62 useful 63 P/proof   64 sunshine
65 daily

Paper 4 Listening (40 minutes approximately)

Part 1
1 A   2 B   3 C   4 A   5 C   6 B   7 A   8 A

Part 2
9 (fairly/very) late   10 discovery/discovering centre   11 feel box
12 careful   13 activity day(s)   14 our planet
15 environment(al) (issues)   16 (a guided) tour   17 (a) tea party
18 (a bag of) gift(s)

Part 3
19 F   20 D   21 A   22 C   23 E

Part 4
24 T   25 T   26 T   27 F   28 F   29 F   30 F

Transcript *First Certificate Listening Test. Test One.*

Hello. I'm going to give you the instructions for this test. I'll introduce each part of the test and give you time to look at the questions. At the start of each piece you'll hear this sound.

tone

You'll hear each piece twice.

Remember, while you're listening, write your answers on the question paper. You'll have time at the end of the test to copy your answers onto the separate answer sheet.

The tape will now be stopped. Please ask any questions now, because you must not speak during the test.

[pause]

PART 1 *Now open your question paper and look at Part One.*

[pause]

You'll hear people talking in eight different situations. For questions 1 to 8, choose the best answer, A, B or C.

Question 1 *One*
You hear a young man talking to his friend about a film. What is his opinion of the film?
A It was too long.
B The acting was poor.
C There was too much violence.

[pause]

tone

Man: ... mm ... well, no, I can't say I really enjoyed it at all that much. I don't go to the cinema much, but I did make the effort for this, because I'd quite enjoyed the book even though I thought it was a bit violent.

Friend: Oh, is it?

Man: Mm, though they'd cut out a lot of that in the film.

Friend: Ah.

Man: Yes ... It had some good people in it and they did their best – you couldn't blame the actors – but honestly it went on and on, by the time it finally ended, I was just longing to get out and have a cup of coffee to wake me up!

[pause]

tone

[The recording is repeated.]

[pause]

Question 2   Two
You hear part of an interview with a man on the radio. What is the man talking about?
A shopping
B gardening
C painting

[pause]

tone

Interviewer: . . . and how about the apples?
Man: Oh, yes – wonderful, and quite easy, too. Some varieties are better than others, of course. It depends what size, colour and texture you're looking for in the apples themselves and obviously the size and shape of the tree are important, too, according to where you want to put it. It's a question of proportion. But nothing beats your own apples – you'll never get them from the supermarket again!

[pause]

tone

[The recording is repeated.]

[pause]

Question 3   Three
You hear a man talking about his job. Where does he work?
A in a hotel
B in a travel agent's
C in a shop

[pause]

tone

Man: Well, we get a lot of tourists from Europe, and Japan, and then we also get a lot of people from cities outside of New York. And then we also get a lot of New Yorkers and people who are very fashion-conscious and very well-to-do. And then we also get customers who are people who normally don't dress this way but they find a certain piece that really excites them. Like if they see a certain shirt or a certain skirt and then just say 'Oh, this is wonderful' and they'll have to get it.

[pause]

tone

[The recording is repeated.]

[pause]

113

Question 4   *Four*
You hear Jessica telling a friend about a trip. Why is she going to Japan?
A to do some painting
B to learn Japanese
C to study Japanese art

[pause]

tone

Male:	Japan! Sounds exciting. Business or pleasure, Jessica?
Jessica:	Well, *some* pleasure, but the trip's being paid for, so it's really business.
Male:	Did you win a scholarship or something?
Jessica:	No, although I expect or, rather, I hope I'll learn some Japanese while I'm there, but in fact this language school in Tokyo wants me to do a big picture in each of eight rooms to show English life and scenery.

[pause]

tone

[The recording is repeated.]

[pause]

Question 5   *Five*
In a hospital waiting room, you hear this conversation. What is the man doing?
A making a complaint
B expressing approval
C making a suggestion

[pause]

tone

Male:	Excuse me. Have you got a minute? Um ... I've been waiting for ages and I was wondering ...
Female:	The doctors *are* very busy ...
Male:	No, no, no, it's not that. It's just that I'm rather thirsty after all this time. Have you thought of getting a drinks machine put in?
Female:	Uhm. I'll speak to the hospital management about that. I don't think so actually.

[pause]

tone

[The recording is repeated.]

[pause]

Question 6	*Six*

Six
You hear some friends talking. How does the woman feel?
A worried
B annoyed
C disappointed

[pause]

tone

Woman:	Look, it's already eight o'clock and Tom said he'd be here by seven.
Man:	Yes, but you know what the traffic is like at this time of the evening.
Woman:	He said he'd make a special effort not to be late. Why does he always do this?
Man:	Keep your hair on. There's probably a reasonable explanation.
Woman:	You mean he'll give us one of his typical excuses. Well, I've had enough this time.

[pause]

tone

[The recording is repeated.]

[pause]

Question 7   *Seven*
You overhear two people talking in a café. What is the relationship between them?
A They belong to the same club.
B They are students together.
C They work for the same company.

[pause]

tone

Man 1:	It's good to get out and do something active at lunchtimes, isn't it?
Man 2:	Yeah, I look forward to our games. And the courts and stuff are pretty good, aren't they, considering how little it costs to join.
Man 1:	Yeah, I'm glad we decided to, of course. I'm still learning but I'll beat you one day!
Man 2:	Oh yeah? Anyway, I'd better get back, I've got to give a talk this afternoon.
Man 1:	Yeah, I've been meaning to ask you, what's it like at your place these days?
Man 2:	Much like yours I should think, dead boring. It's not what I thought I'd end up doing when I was at college.

[pause]

tone

[The recording is repeated.]

[pause]

Question 8   *Eight*
You hear part of a radio programme on the subject of films. What is special about the music in John Hunt's film?
A It holds your attention.
B It follows the action.
C It stays in your memory.

[pause]

tone

Man: Film music is like another voice which is telling you part of the story. Certain types are given names, like 'Mickey Mousing', for example, where the music directly follows the action on the screen. The films of John Hunt, however, are known for their minimalist music, which is three or four notes in repetition, a great deal of repetition, and, after a while, this begins to work on the emotions of the audience and as you're sitting in the cinema you get tense and more involved in what's going on on the screen.

[pause]

tone

[The recording is repeated.]

[pause]

That is the end of Part One.

Now turn to Part Two.

PART 2   *You'll hear part of a nature programme for young people in Britain. For questions 9 to 18, fill in the missing information.*

You now have forty-five seconds in which to look at Part Two.

[pause]

tone

Kathy: OK, now it's time for our regular slot 'Nature Notes', and as usual Paul Sinclair is here to tell us about some of the things you can look out for at the moment. Paul, I believe the Natural History Museum in London has something of particular interest at the moment.

Paul: Yes, they have. They've got what they call 'Dinosaur Safari', which is an exhibition that takes you back to the time when those pre-historic creatures were around. With the use of high technology, they've created some realistic moving dinosaurs that can be pretty scary, I warn you! One tip I would give you, though, is to get to the exhibition fairly late to miss the worst of the queues. After all, there's plenty more to see in the museum before that.

Kathy: What about for people who can't get to London for that?

Paul: Yes, for those of you out of easy reach of London, the Museum also has something called the Discovery Centre, which visits venues around the country and is particularly aimed at young people. One great thing is that they have specimens you can touch such as bones and stuffed animals. And one thing that's proved particularly popular is known as the 'feel box' where you identify mystery objects by touch only. So try to get along to the centre when it comes to your area.

Kathy: Now, there's something for budding geologists, isn't there?

Paul: Yes, it's a project called 'Rockwatch' and the idea is to encourage young people to be *careful* collectors of rocks. The organisers say that *careless* collecting can easily damage sites and that the youngsters could teach the grown-ups a thing or two about that. Anyone aged between 8 and 18 can join Rockwatch, which will give them a chance to learn about fossils, dinosaurs and so on. And also they'll be able to go along to activity days, where they can take part in all sorts of exciting things.

Kathy: You've got something about a writing competition next, haven't you?

Paul: Yes, that's right, it's called 'Our Planet'. It's being run by the Society for the Protection of Birds and it's open to anyone up to the age of 20. They've called it 'Our Planet' because it doesn't just concern birds. It can be anything to do with the environment. If you want to enter, you have to write a 400-word article on an environmental issue that's close to your heart and send it to them before July 30. The prize is certainly well worth having – a word processor that will be great for anyone who's keen to be a writer.

Kathy: OK, and finally, exciting things are happening at Edinburgh Zoo, aren't they?

Paul: They certainly are. On June 18th, they're holding an open day for young people. You'll get a guided tour in the morning and there'll be quizzes and demonstrations during the afternoon. After that there's a tea party at one of the city's biggest hotels, which should be great fun. Tickets cost £10 and for that you also get a bag of gifts, so it's well worth the money.

Kathy: OK, thanks Paul. You can get details of everything that ...

[pause]

tone

Now you'll hear Part Two again.

[The recording is repeated.]

[pause]

That's the end of Part Two.

Now turn to Part Three.

PART 3   *You will hear five people talking about experiences connected with school. For questions 19 to 23, choose from the list A to F what each speaker says about his or her school days. Use the letters only once. There is one extra letter which you do not need to use.*

You now have thirty seconds in which to look at Part Three.

[pause]

tone

Speaker 1:   It may have a great reputation, especially for football, but I only went there because my parents insisted I had to go. I met a lot of people who've been useful to me in later life, but apart from that it was a waste of time for me. I suppose I enjoyed the woodwork, but if they thought I was going to make an effort, they were wrong.

Speaker 2:   We moved from another part of the country, and I arrived in the middle of term. Everyone already had their friends, and I felt left out of everything. But Mike Trenchard really helped. He taught modern languages – which I was good at – and he really helped me fit in, despite my failures on the tennis court. I remember . . .

Speaker 3:   I wasn't really any good at things like history and maths. The one thing I did enjoy was swimming so I got chosen for the team in my first term – and then I had the confidence to try other things like fencing and athletics, and I ended up being a bit of a star.

Speaker 4:   My parents were both teachers and I was very interested in books but the school seemed more interested in training girls in cookery and needlework, where I was just hopeless. I wanted to study Latin and Greek but everyone – teachers especially – thought I was odd. I couldn't wait to leave.

Speaker 5:   It was in the fifth year, the year when we had to study really hard, and there was this boy whose brother was going out with my sister and he started spreading rumours, saying things about my parents and me. And my work was suffering and in the end the school authorities had to sort it out.

[pause]

tone

Now you'll hear Part Three again.

[The recording is repeated.]

[pause]

That's the end of Part Three.

Now turn to Part Four.

PART 4   *You will hear part of a radio interview with a famous Australian novelist, Dorothy Shields. For questions 24 to 30, decide which of the statements are TRUE and which are FALSE. Write T for True or F for False in the box provided.*

You now have forty-five seconds in which to look at Part Four.

[pause]

tone

Interviewer: You've just finished writing your life story, haven't you?

Dorothy: Well, Volume One actually, and I don't see how there can ever be a Volume Two because of the number of people I've known who are still alive. Now, the book I've just finished, is about people most of whom are dead or don't care.

Interviewer: So, you don't believe in giving away other people's secrets?

Dorothy: No, I absolutely do not.

Interviewer: I suppose the other reason for writing your life story is that if you don't, other people will do it for you, and, as long as you're around and able to write it yourself, it must be very annoying if they want to.

Dorothy: Well, there is a young woman writing one now. I tried to stop her, but I've given up. I thought, 'OK, if you can't beat them, join them' so that's why I wrote my book, yes.

Interviewer: But also annoying if you're capable of doing it yourself is that, however well researched it is, it's bound to be inaccurate, to a certain extent, isn't it?

Dorothy:	I also think they make things up quite a lot. Sometimes I think 'Oh, it doesn't matter', but, you know, at other times I get quite cross. But I don't know if this book is to improve things or not, because I don't know what people are expecting really.
Interviewer:	But you also tore up your first two novels, didn't you?
Dorothy:	I've torn up a lot more than that. Yes, I ripped them up and a lot of short stories too.
Interviewer:	You've gone on tearing them up?
Dorothy:	I tore one up last year actually. You know it's much better to start again than to try and change something, you see. Because you get on to a sort of, um … well, I don't know, a wavelength when it's going well.
Interviewer:	But if you decide that you really should begin again, why don't you just put it away somewhere, you never know, if you've spent that long working on it, isn't it a terrible thing just to throw it away?
Dorothy:	Well, if I do have a moment of doubt afterwards, I think of all the theses that might be written about it and then I'm pleased that it's not going to be studied!
Interviewer:	But, when you first came to this country, as an adult, with the manuscript of what was to be your first published novel in your suitcase, it was published and met with immediate success. Were you surprised?
Dorothy:	Well, you know, I was a very raw young woman out of the bush then. I've now become elderly and respectable, but then I was so green and when publishers phoned me up to say it had been accepted, I thought 'this must be what happens to everybody'. They saw me as extremely cool, but really I just didn't know.
Interviewer:	But, you believed you would be published?
Dorothy:	Yes, I find it very difficult now to understand my state of mind at that time. My confidence was amazing. I just knew I was going to be a writer and I was going to be published. There's a phrase that's disappeared, a 1950s phrase, 'to be in for the long haul'. I was always in for the long haul, I wasn't going to give up and turn my hand to anything else, because, well as I say, what could I do?

[pause]

tone

Now you'll hear Part Four again.

[The recording is repeated.]

[pause]

That's the end of Part Four.

There'll now be a pause of five minutes for you to copy your answers onto the separate answer sheet.
I'll remind you when there is one minute left, so that you're sure to finish in time.

[pause]

You have one more minute left.

[pause]

That's the end of the test. Please stop now. Your supervisor will now collect all the question papers and answer sheets.
Goodbye.

Test 2 Key

Paper 1   Reading (1 hour 15 minutes)

Part 1
1 C   2 F   3 E   4 A   5 H   6 B   7 G

Part 2
8 D   9 D   10 B   11 A   12 D   13 B   14 C   15 B

Part 3
16 F   17 H   18 G   19 B   20 C   21 E   22 A

Part 4
23 A   24 C   25 B   26 A   27 B   28 D   29 A   30 B
31 B   32 D   33 C   34 A   35 C

Paper 2   Writing (1 hour 30 minutes)

Task-specific mark schemes

Question 1

Content
Major points: Early explanation of who is writing and why i.e. requesting permission to hold a party. Must give precise information – date, time, place. Some reference needed to noise and tidying up.
Minor points: who is responsible for what (Noriko, Amanda).

Organisation and cohesion
Clear opening to letter. Suitable paragraphing. Appropriate ending.

Appropriacy of register and format
Formal letter.

Range
Language of requests. Language of description and future plans. Some expression of persuasion/reassurance. Vocabulary relating to the organisation of parties.

Target reader
Would have enough information to consider the request.

Question 2

Content
Letter should include brief reference to fact that the cousin was not able to come to the wedding. Coverage of the whole day's events. Some details of the guests.

Range
Language of description for events and people. Past tenses. Vocabulary relating to wedding celebrations.

Organisation and cohesion
Clear opening to letter. Suitable paragraphing. Appropriate ending.

Appropriacy of register and format
Informal letter.

Target reader
Would have a picture of the wedding and be informed about who was there.

Question 3

Content
Story related in some way to the first day, beginning with the words given.

Range
Narrative. Past tenses. Language of description.

Organisation and cohesion
Opening sentences set the scene. Possibly only minimal paragraphing thereafter. Obvious ending.

Appropriacy of register and format
Consistently neutral or informal.

Target reader
Would be able to follow the storyline.

Question 4

Content
Suggestions of ways to remember new vocabulary in English. More than one suggestion must be given.

Range
Language of opinion and suggestion. Use of appropriate modals. Vocabulary relating to language learning.

Organisation and cohesion
Clear opening to article. Suitable paragraphing. Conclusion.

Appropriacy of register and format
More or less formal (written for college magazine) but must be consistent.

Target reader
Would be informed.

Question 5(a)

Content
Clear reference to the book. Description of two pictures and an explanation as to why they would make a suitable cover.

Range
Language of description and explanation.

Organisation and cohesion
Linking of description and explanation.

Appropriacy of register and format
Neutral. Composition layout.

Target reader
Would know why the writer thinks these two pictures would make a suitable cover.

Question 5(b)

Content
Clear reference to the book chosen. Description of the character chosen and the change(s) undergone.

Range
Language of description, opinion and explanation.

Organisation and cohesion
Linking of description, opinion and explanation.

Appropriacy of register and format
Neutral. Composition layout.

Target reader
Would understand why the writer has chosen this character.

Paper 3 Use of English (1 hour 15 minutes)

Part 1

1 A   2 D   3 B   4 B   5 C   6 D   7 C   8 B   9 D
10 A   11 C   12 A   13 C   14 D   15 B

Part 2

16 which/that   17 used   18 could/can   19 to   20 become
21 until/till/before   22 first   23 had/made/created   24 how
25 where   26 because/as/since   27 on   28 their   29 for   30 the

Part 3

Award one mark for each correct section.
31 enjoyed the film (1) apart from (1)
32 is going to (1) be pulled (1)

33 has been learning Russian (1) for (1)
34 told/instructed/commanded/ordered Rebecca (1) not to (1) OR said (that)
   Rebecca (1) must/should not (1)
35 was not/wasn't (1) as/so expensive/dear/costly as (1)
36 there was (1) no point (in) (1)
37 must (1) have/'ve been (1)
38 did not/didn't deserve (1) to be (1)
39 nothing left (1) in this/the (1)
40 was forty/40 (1) when he learned/learnt/started/began (1)

Part 4

41 as   42 ✓   43 it   44 ✓   45 go   46 so   47 the
48 they   49 to   50 ✓   51 of   52 that   53 much   54 kind
55 who

Part 5

56 carefully   57 organisations   58 majority   59 cultural
60 knowledge   61 teenagers   62 correspondence   63 obligation
64 entertainment   65 broaden

Paper 4   Listening (40 minutes approximately)

Part 1
1 B   2 B   3 B   4 A   5 C   6 A   7 C   8 C

Part 2

9 (a) painter/(an) artist   10 (the) (old) bus station
11 (a) golf champion/(champion) golfer   12 (a) furniture shop
13 engineering   14 (the) Market Hall
15 Nothing Ever Changes   16 (a) bank robbery   17 (the) Leisure Centre
18 (the) Evening Post/(the/our) local evening (news)paper

Part 3
19 F   20 D   21 A   22 E   23 B

Part 4
24 T   25 T   26 F   27 F   28 T   29 T   30 F

Transcript   *First Certificate Listening Test. Test Two.*
Hello. I'm going to give you the instructions for this test. I'll introduce each
part of the test and give you time to look at the questions. At the start of
each piece you'll hear this sound.

tone

You will hear each piece twice.

Remember, while you're listening, write your answers on the question paper. You'll have time at the end of the test to copy your answers onto the separate answer sheet.

The tape will now be stopped. Please ask any questions now, because you must not speak during the test.

[pause]

PART 1   *Now open your question paper and look at Part One.*

[pause]

You will hear people talking in eight different situations. For questions 1 to 8, choose the best answer, A, B or C.

Question 1   *One*
You hear two people discussing a play. Who is going to see it?
A the man
B both of them
C neither of them

[pause]

tone

Man: ... well, I'm not sure. It sounds as if it might be rather violent for us.
Woman: Yes, but it's ever so famous. The director won some kind of award. Peter saw it a few months ago and according to him some of it *was* violent, but it was all done in a very matter-of-fact way – nothing too ... um ... you know ...
Man: OK, then. I suppose it'll make a change from comedies.

[pause]

tone

[The recording is repeated.]

[pause]

Question 2   *Two*
You will hear an announcement about a television programme. What is the programme about?
A Indian religion
B Indian cooking
C Indian history

[pause]

tone

Announcer: ... and at 8.30 there's another chance to see the last in our series 'Indian Magic'. In tonight's programme, Usha Verma travels to central India and tries some of the dishes prepared by this historic region's top cooks. She will also be giving you once again a step-by-step guide to producing similar delights at home and looking at some of the traditional dishes associated with a festival at a famous local temple.

[pause]

tone

[The recording is repeated.]

[pause]

Question 3   *Three*
Listen to this man speaking. Who is he?
A a traffic policeman
B a taxi driver
C a tour guide

[pause]

tone

Man: Well I can, but the traffic may be bad when we get nearer the centre. You'll have to walk the last hundred metres or so anyway, because I'm not allowed to stop outside the theatre. I've got into a lot of trouble recently for trying to do that. You can get out at Brammel Lane and it's just round the corner. You won't get lost.

[pause]

tone

[The recording is repeated.]

[pause]

Question 4   *Four*
In a hotel, the receptionist is giving a guest his bill. What is the problem?
A The man has made a mistake.
B It is someone else's bill.
C There is a mistake in the bill.

[pause]

tone

Receptionist: That's £125.97 altogether then, sir.
Guest: All right. Let me see. What's this? I'm sorry but, I made *one* phone call, not two. I've been charged for two calls. This is my bill, I suppose?
Receptionist: Why, yes, and the calls are automatically recorded by computer. I can't see how . . .
Guest: Oh, wait a minute. Yes, I did make a quick call to a friend last night. That would be it. Sorry.

[pause]

tone

[The recording is repeated.]

[pause]

Question 5 Five
You hear someone talking on a public phone. Who is he talking to?
A a friend
B a repair man
C a taxi company

[pause]

tone

Man: . . . look, you told me you'd pick me up in 10 to 15 minutes when I first rang but that was half an hour ago. I've been waiting outside this phone box all that time and it's freezing cold . . . What do you mean, it came and there was nobody here so it went away again? I've been here all the time, I haven't moved. Look, you're obviously unreliable, and I've got a plane to catch . . . No, no, I'll phone another firm.

[pause]

tone

[The recording is repeated.]

[pause]

Question 6 Six
In a museum café you overhear two people talking. What did the woman feel about the exhibition?
A She was impressed.
B She was disappointed.
C She was bored.

[pause]

tone

Female: . . . actually, it wasn't quite what I expected.
Man: Yes, I thought there'd be more variety.
Female: No, that's not what I meant. I didn't expect the colours to be so striking, it was so original.
Man: Yes, that's true – but the theme was so limited.
Female: I didn't mind. Where can I see more of his work?

[pause]

tone

[The recording is repeated.]

[pause]

Question 7 Seven
You hear a woman telephoning a furniture store. What does she want the store to do?
A deliver her table on Tuesday
B leave the table at her neighbour's house
C confirm the delivery time

[pause]

tone

Woman: Yes, good morning. I'm enquiring about the table I ordered a couple of weeks ago ...
Mrs James, 58 West Street ... So when can you deliver it? ... Next Tuesday? OK ...
No, hang on, that won't do ... Thursday? Should be OK. If I'm not here, my
neighbour could let you in. Will it be morning or afternoon? ... Well, if you could let
me know definitely ... Fine. Thank you ... Bye.

[pause]

tone

[The recording is repeated.]

[pause]

Question 8   *Eight*
You hear two people in a travel agent's arguing about a trip. What do they
disagree about?
A whether to go or not
B how much it will cost
C when to go

[pause]

tone

Female: Look, I thought we'd agreed all this.
Male: Yes, but you heard what the assistant said – it can get unbearably hot there then.
Female: So what are you saying, you don't want to go? Look, I've already put my name down
at work for those weeks and I don't want to have to change it.
Male: I'm just saying we shouldn't go *then*, that's all. It won't be any more expensive if we
leave it until a bit later. Surely you could get them to put it back a bit ...

[pause]

tone

[The recording is repeated.]

[pause]

That is the end of Part One.

Now turn to Part Two.

PART 2   *You will hear part of a local radio programme, in which the presenters give*
the answers to a quiz. For questions 9 to 18, fill in the answers to the quiz.

You now have forty-five seconds in which to look at Part Two.

[pause]

tone

Male:	... right, now it's time for the answers to last week's local history quiz. Carol, would you like to start?
Female:	OK, the first question was 'Who was Alexander Byfleet?' Did you know this one, Phil?
Male:	Well, I was sure he was an inventor. I didn't know we'd had any artists living here.
Female:	Well, that's what he was – painted some rather pretty pictures actually.
Male:	OK, next we asked you 'What used to be where the Buy Easy Supermarket is now?' There was some confusion over this one, wasn't there?
Female:	Mmm. Some people wrote the old police station and some said the old bus station, which is what it was. The old police station was further down the road.
Male:	The next question was 'Who was Jimmy Milburn, who lived here all his life?' This was a bit of a tricky one, wasn't it?
Female:	Yes, quite a few people fell into the trap and put 'professional footballer', but that was Johnny his brother.
Male:	In fact Jimmy was a golf champion – he won the national championships for five years running in the 1940s.
Female:	OK. Then we asked 'There was once a boot factory in the town. What is it now?' Not many people knew this one, did they?
Male:	No, including me! Well, apparently it was in Dean Road and when it closed it was used as a garage for a while before it became a furniture shop.
Female:	Which is what it currently is.
Male:	The next question was 'A hundred years ago, what was the town's main industry?' Well, the obvious answer was 'clothes-making' ...
Female:	... yes, because of course that's what the town has a reputation for today. So it may come as a surprise to many of you that there was more engineering than anything else in those days ...
Male:	... Uh huh.
Female:	We then asked 'What is the oldest building in the town?' A lot of you went for the Children's Hospital and, of course, the church. But, the church was completely rebuilt 150 years ago and the hospital is not quite as old as the Market Hall, which was built in 1672. Phil.
Male:	The next question was 'Anthony Diprose wrote a novel that was set in the town. What is that novel called?' Well, it wasn't a best seller so perhaps it's not so surprising that hardly anyone knew that the title of the book was 'Nothing Ever Changes'.
Female:	Then we asked 'What happened in Wood Lane in 1976 that was in all the national newspapers?' Well, plenty of people remembered there was a flood there in the mid-70s.
Male:	Yes, although as those of you who were actually living here in 1976 may recall, that was the year of our famous bank robbery ...
Female:	The flood happened in '77 by the way.
Male:	The next question was 'Which public building was opened in 1985?' The new Town Hall was a popular answer and many of you put the Shopping Centre. Well, in fact they're both a bit older than that, believe it or not. It was the Leisure Centre that first came into use that year.
Female:	That surprised me. Anyway, finally, we asked 'What celebrates its hundredth anniversary this year?' The football club got a lot of votes here – it's been around longer than that! As many of you thought, it's our local newspaper, the Evening Post, which was first published 100 years ago.
Male:	OK, now for the winners.

[pause]

tone

Now you'll hear Part Two again.

[The recording is repeated.]

[pause]

That's the end of Part Two.

Now turn to Part Three.

PART 3   *You will hear five people talking on the radio about their jobs. For questions 19 to 23, choose from the list A to F how each got his or her job originally. Use the letters only once. There is one extra letter which you do not need to use.*

You now have thirty seconds in which to look at Part Three.

[pause]

tone

Speaker 1:   Well, I didn't really have the qualifications for the job, at least not on paper, but anyway, I got an interview, which was absolute hell, and afterwards I thought "Well, it was worth a try", but I was sure I hadn't got it. Then, a couple of days later, they rang up and offered it to me. You know, it was only a few weeks later I found out that they'd intended to give it to someone else with the same surname, and I'd been second on the list. But I'm still there, so I suppose I'm OK.

[pause]

Speaker 2:   I've always loved selling and marketing and had several jobs doing that before this particular job. You know, it's strange how life is really because I very nearly didn't work here. Mr Kelly, he's the director, offered me the job at the interview, and I turned it down but he rang me again a few days later to see if I'd been having second thoughts. I had, I'm glad to say.

[pause]

Speaker 3:   My motorbike broke down. And I had to wait around while it was being repaired. Yeah, so I bought a local paper and went into a café and read it and happened to see the advert for the job. I thought, "I'll have a go at that", and rang up. It was just down the road and they said, "Come along right away". I knew absolutely nothing about this line of work then, but they must have liked my face at the interview or something.

[pause]

Speaker 4:   Never be late for a job interview because you won't get the job! I ever so nearly was. Would you believe it? The train broke down on the way. There I was – stuck miles from where I was going. But actually we were in a station, and I realised I'd never make the interview and got off the train. Well, I got talking to someone outside and they offered me a lift and I arrived early for the interview, in the end.

[pause]

Speaker 5:   They rang up and offered me the job, and I was really thankful, because I'd been out of work for ages, and was beginning to think I'd never get anything. What I now know is that I was the only person who turned up for interview. Apparently a couple of other people were asked but never came. So I kind of got it because they had no choice, although they could have advertised it again, I suppose. Glad they didn't.

[pause]

tone

Now you'll hear Part Three again.

[The recording is repeated.]

[pause]

That's the end of Part Three.

Now turn to Part Four.

PART 4   *You will hear a young actress being interviewed on the radio. Answer questions 24 to 30, by writing T for True or F for False in the boxes provided.*

You now have thirty seconds in which to look at Part Four.

[pause]

tone

Interviewer:	We have in the studio today, Beatrice Rand. A gifted young actress, well known to all of you for her starring role in *To Fly with the Wind* and whose next film is due out this summer.
Beatrice:	Thank you.
Interviewer:	I'd like to begin, if I may, by asking you about how it all started. Why an actress?
Beatrice:	Oh, I've always wanted to be an actress. Or at least I've always wanted to perform. When I was very young, our neighbour used to play the piano all day every day. My parents hated it. They complained about it all the time. I couldn't understand why – I loved listening to him. It fascinated me. I wanted to be able to do it.
Interviewer:	But you didn't start with music did you? In fact, wasn't your first love the circus?
Beatrice:	Yes, my father made a circus area in our back garden with swings and ropes and things and I used to practise for hours. When I was seven I telephoned a circus school. They told me I had to wait until I was ten.
Interviewer:	What did you do then?
Beatrice:	For the time being I decided to be an actress. I was in all the school plays and I joined a local dramatic society – you know – only small things. I just wanted to perform. I used to imagine myself in front of huge audiences.
Interviewer:	You had a very lively imagination when you were young.
Beatrice:	Oh yes. I invented a completely imaginary life when I was about eight years old. And the most important part of my imaginary life was a friend called Elizabeth.
Interviewer:	Do you think that was because you were lonely?
Beatrice:	Not really. I had lots of school friends, but real friends can't be with you all the time. An imaginary friend can, and I could talk to Elizabeth whenever I wanted to. She was always there.
Interviewer:	Did she encourage your desire to be an actress?

Beatrice:	Oh yes. She was always in the audience and she always told me when I'd done well and when I'd done badly.
Interviewer:	So by the time you left school you were already quite an experienced actress. In fact, at sixteen you were quite mature for your age.
Beatrice:	Yes, I suppose I was. I knew what I wanted to do when I was quite young and by the time I was sixteen I was well on the way to achieving it.
Interviewer:	Did you have any other interests when you were young?
Beatrice:	Well, I used to love reading. I read hundreds of books when I was young and I loved poetry. I knew a lot of poems by heart. I've always been very good at remembering words.
Interviewer:	And now that you're a successful actress, how do you feel about what you've achieved?
Beatrice:	I'm glad to be doing what I always wanted to do. But there are problems that I never thought about.
Interviewer:	Such as?
Beatrice:	Well, it's difficult to enjoy going to restaurants or discos and things like that. I wanted to improve my dancing. But going to dance classes wouldn't have been easy with everyone staring at you.
Interviewer:	And I believe your career is about to take another direction.

[pause]

tone

Now you'll hear Part Four again.

[The recording is repeated.]

[pause]

That's the end of Part Four.

There'll now be a pause of five minutes for you to copy your answers onto the separate answer sheet. I'll remind you when there is one minute left, so that you're sure to finish in time.

[pause]

You have one more minute left.

[pause]

That's the end of the test. Please stop now. Your supervisor will now collect all the question papers and answer sheets.
Goodbye.

Test 3 Key

Paper 1   Reading (1 hour 15 minutes)

Part 1
1 E   2 H   3 G   4 C   5 D   6 A   7 B

Part 2
8 C   9 D   10 D   11 A   12 B   13 A   14 D   15 C

Part 3
16 G   17 E   18 B   19 F   20 A   21 C

Part 4
22 H   23 A   24 B   25 C   26 A   27 E   28 H   29 E
30/31 I/D (*in any order*)   32 G   33 F   34/35 A/F (*in any order*)

Paper 2   Writing (1 hour 30 minutes)

Task-specific mark schemes

Question 1
Content
Major points: State city to go to and when. Ask for a guide. Request information re being met at the airport and which hotel.
Minor points: Any requests for special arrangements. Any comment on spending allowance or meals.

Organisation and cohesion
Letter with appropriate opening and closing formulae. Clear organisation of points: statement of needs, questions and requests. Appropriate linking of ideas – not just lists.

Appropriacy of register and format
Letter format. Could range from neutral to formal, but must be consistent throughout.

Range
Language of requests and questions. Range of tenses: possibly future, present, conditionals. Vocabulary to do with travel and holidays. Some lifting of key words/phrases acceptable e.g. *special arrangements*.

Target reader
Would know what the writer specifically wants and have enough information to make the appropriate arrangements.

Question 2

Content
Give advice about how to learn the candidate's language. State main difficulties. NB Also acceptable to expand on *one* main area of difficulty.

Range
Language for giving factual information, suggestions and advice. Probably present and future forms. Possibly conditionals and modals. Vocabulary to do with language learning.

Organisation and cohesion
Early reference to reason for writing. Clear organisation and linking of points. Suitable opening and closing formulae.

Appropriacy of register and format
Informal letter.

Target reader
Will have a clear idea as to how to start learning the language and what difficulties to expect.

Question 3

Content
Story which makes context of '*playing*' clear. What happened next, and with what result.

Range
Range of past tenses. Language of narration and description. Vocabulary appropriate to the context chosen.

Organisation and cohesion
Could be minimally paragraphed. Ideas linked and developed, leading from the given prompt to a specified outcome.

Appropriacy of register and format
Neutral or informal register possible, but must be consistent throughout.

Target reader
Would be able to follow the storyline.

Question 4

Content
Recommendations specific to a bookshop. Explanation as to why recommendations would prove popular with young people.

Range
Language of description and recommendation. Possibly present, future and conditionals. Vocabulary to do with shops and the likes or dislikes of young people.

Organisation and cohesion
Report should be clearly organised. Sub-headings an advantage. Report may possibly begin in letter format. Clearly stated recommendations.

Appropriacy of register and format
Register could range from neutral to formal, but must be consistent throughout.
Formal report layout not essential.

Target reader
Would have a clear idea of what the recommendations are and why they should
prove popular.

Question 5(a)
Content
State which book. Describe the scene. Explain why this scene is the one to film.

Range
Language of description, explanation and justification. Range of tenses.
Vocabulary relating to the specific scene chosen.

Organisation and cohesion
Logical linking between the description and the reasons for filming.

Appropriacy of register and format
Composition. Range of register appropriate, provided consistent.

Target reader
Would learn about the scene from the book in some detail and why it would be
good to film.

Question 5(b)
Content
State which book. Agree or disagree with the proposition, or discuss both sides
of the argument. Give reasons for the view. Explain this view with reference to
the book.

Range
Language of opinion, explanation, and justification. Range of tenses.
Vocabulary to do with books and language learning.

Organisation and cohesion
Clear development of viewpoint with appropriate linking of ideas.

Appropriacy of register and format
Composition. Range of register appropriate, provided consistent.

Target reader
Would know which book the writer had read and whether the reading of books
is seen as an aid to studying English.

Paper 3 Use of English (1 hour 15 minutes)

Part 1

1 B	2 A	3 A	4 B	5 A	6 B	7 C	8 D	9 C
10 A	11 C	12 D	13 D	14 B	15 A			

Part 2

16 it   17 to   18 they   19 was   20 a   21 this/that   22 have
23 for   24 be   25 than   26 which/that   27 as   28 the
29 one   30 had

Part 3

Award one mark for each correct section.
31 last time/occasion (when/that) (1) I saw (1)
32 is included (1) in (1)
33 taken the/his car (1) without asking (1)
34 had/'d better (1) get/have (1)
35 not like Sarah (1) to be (1)
36 want anyone/body else (1) to know (1)
37 was cancelled (1) owing to (1)
38 in case (1) the taxi is (1)
39 too fast/quickly (1) for them to (1)
40 gave me (1) (his/her) permission (1) OR gave (1) (his/her) permission for me (1)

Part 4

41 by   42 of   43 will   44 ✓   45 to   46 the   47 it
48 ✓   49 ✓   50 in   51 ✓   52 those   53 quite
54 ✓   55 other

Part 5

56 unemployment   57 construction   58 shortly
59 announcement(s)   60 advertising   61 qualified   62 intention
63 recently   64 enthusiastic   65 wealthy

Paper 4   Listening (40 minutes approximately)

Part 1

1 C   2 C   3 A   4 B   5 A   6 C   7 C   8 C

Part 2

9 camera equipment
10 up to 4/1–4/no more than 4/a max(imum) (of) 4/four
11 everyday objects *not* things like a bowl of fruit, etc.
12 (some)scenery/view(s) *not* view(s) from windows, etc.
13 comedy/amusing scenes (in home/at work)
14/15 (the/a)negative(s)/(a) (short) description (*in any order*)
16 Amateur Photography   17 picture editor   18 April (issue/magazine)

Part 3

19 B   20 E   21 A   22 F   23 C

Part 4

24 C   **25** N   **26** N   **27** B   **28** C   **29** C   **30** B

Transcript   *First Certificate Listening Test. Test Three.*

Hello. I'm going to give you the instructions for this test. I'll introduce each part of the test and give you time to look at the questions. At the start of each piece you'll hear this sound.

tone

You'll hear each piece twice.

Remember, while you're listening, write your answers on the question paper. You'll have time at the end of the test to copy your answers onto the separate answer sheet.

The tape will now be stopped. Please ask any questions now, because you must not speak during the test.

[pause]

PART 1   *Now open your question paper and look at Part One.*

[pause]

You will hear people talking in eight different situations. For questions 1 to 8, choose the best answer, A, B or C.

Question 1   One
Listen to this girl talking about a book she has just read. What does she think about the book?
A It is inaccurate.
B It is depressing.
C It is too long.

[pause]

tone

Woman: Hi, James. You can have your book back now. I finished it last night – finally. It took me ages to read. I liked the bits when he described his adventures in the mountains – they were really amazing. But I think he could have left out some of the descriptive passages. I'd have finished the book ages ago if he had.

[pause]

tone

[The recording is repeated.]

[pause]

Question 2   Two
You hear a woman talking to a man. What is she doing?

A complaining about something
B suggesting something
C explaining something

[pause]

Man:	Did you remember to bring the tennis balls?
Woman:	No, I didn't ...
Man:	What! I thought you said you'd bring some. How are we going to play without them?
Woman:	Well, the ones I had were very old and I know you'd only get cross if we played with them. So I phoned Janet. She's just bought some new tennis balls. She'll be along in a few minutes then we'll be able to play.

[pause]

tone

[The recording is repeated.]

[pause]

Question 3 *Three*
You overhear a woman talking about somewhere she visited on holiday.
What is she describing?
A a palace
B an art gallery
C a department store

[pause]

tone

Woman:	... oh yes, it was absolutely fascinating. They've got all these old family portraits on the walls and the rooms are full of beautiful furniture and, you know, exotic carpets and things. And there are vases and clocks and that sort of thing too ... Oh, and a marvellous collection of old toys on display in the royal nursery. I really liked that. You could just imagine the little princes and princesses playing with them. Then outside there was a ...

[pause]

tone

[The recording is repeated.]

[pause]

Question 4 *Four*
Listen to this couple talking about a parcel they have received. Why are they disappointed?
A They ordered a different item.
B It is not suitable.
C It has been damaged.

[pause]

tone

Woman:	Right, let's have a look. Oh no!
Man:	What's the matter? Faulty?
Woman:	This is no use.
Man:	Why?
Woman:	I *told* them over the phone what I needed it for and they said this one would do, but it obviously won't. Look!
Man:	Uhm. I see what you mean.

[pause]

tone

[The recording is repeated.]

[pause]

Question 5   *Five*
You hear a local shopkeeper talking about tourists. What is he complaining about?
A the way they treat local people
B the increasing numbers of them
C how little money they spend

[pause]

tone

Man: A few years ago there were hardly any, but now there are more and more every year. They've completely changed the place. I know the local economy couldn't do without them. And I don't mind them coming here, but the attitude of some of them gets on my nerves. They always argue about prices, they seem to think everything should be incredibly cheap. They get quite rude about it sometimes. They've no respect for us at all, some of them.

[pause]

tone

[The recording is repeated.]

[pause]

Question 6   *Six*
You switch on the radio and hear something being read. What is it?
A a weather forecast
B a news report
C a story

[pause]

tone

Man: … and with the wind roaring about his ears and the rain soaking his body, the weary traveller knocked on the door of the dark and unlit cottage. It was with a sinking heart that he waited. Then the door opened. A small elderly woman stood in front of him.

[pause]

tone

[The recording is repeated.]

[pause]

Question 7   *Seven*
You overhear two people talking as they leave their office. What is the
woman going to do this weekend?
A play tennis
B go to the beach
C work in the garden

[pause]

tone

Woman:	Bye, Mark! Have a nice weekend.
Man:	Thanks. Same to you. Doing anything exciting?
Woman:	No, not really. We were thinking of going down to the coast but I don't think Martin's going to be well enough, so he'll probably stay in and watch TV while I get on with planting the rose bushes I bought last weekend. How about you? Playing tennis again?

[pause]

tone

[The recording is repeated.]

[pause]

Question 8   *Eight*
You hear a man talking about his life. How does he feel?
A determined
B hopeful
C regretful

[pause]

tone

Male:	If I could, I would wish that I had a fairly decent job, payin' at least a hundred seventy five or two hundred dollars a week, a nice lady, somebody that would share my life with me, that I could talk to and be with, a place to stay, come home from work and watch TV – that's what I would wish for. Because you know when I was younger, I used to think that a lot of clothes and a lot of money was important. But now I realise that I ain't gonna live for ever so what good is a lot of money if I can't have happiness?

[pause]

tone

[The recording is repeated.]

[pause]

That is the end of Part One.
Now turn to Part Two.

PART 2   *You will hear a magazine editor talking on the radio about a competition.*
For questions 9 to 18, complete the notes.

You now have thirty seconds in which to look at Part Two.

[pause]

tone

Announcer: And now it's time for our weekly magazine feature. I have with me Richard Stevens, editor of 'Amateur Photography'. Richard what's in this month's issue?

Richard: Thanks, Mary. Well, for all those listeners who are keen on taking photographs this may be the competition for you because you *could* win camera equipment to the value of £500 to take your next holiday shots with. Yes, that's first prize in our photography competition. So, here's what it's all about. We're asking anyone who's interested in taking part in this competition to send in up to four photographs. The photos must be five by eight inches – which is a bit larger than normal holiday snaps.

And it's not just any photograph that we're looking for. You must send photographs that fall into one of the following three categories. The first category is photographs of everyday objects – things like, an old chair, some brightly coloured cups and saucers or a bowl of fruit, for example. For the second category, you may choose to photograph some scenery, like the view from a window or a shot of the countryside or the sea. And lastly you could choose to send in a photograph for the comedy category – an amusing scene at work or in the home, for example. You can, of course, have people in these pictures but they won't be the main theme of the picture. So, those are the three types of photograph that you can send in and your entries can be in any of the three groups – there's no ruling about that. What we do insist on is that the pictures are taken by you and so we'll need the negative to prove that as well. And when you send in your entries, please also enclose a short description of the photos so that the judges can be sure of the subject matter and the category for each picture.

Now, you need to send the photographs to 'Amateur Photography' at 21, The Crescent, Ely. The telephone number is 243160 in case you need to ask for any extra information. When all the photographs have been received, they'll be judged during the first week of March by Miranda Smith, our picture editor. I'm afraid I can't give you any more information on that at the moment as we're still finalising details. So you've still got three weeks or so to take the pictures, or enlarge ones that you already have and send them in. The final date for entries is the last day of February and the winners will be announced in our April issue.

Announcer: So what else have you got this month, Richard?

Richard: Well, we've got a special feature . . .

[pause]

tone

Now you'll hear Part Two again.

[The recording is repeated.]

[pause]

That's the end of Part Two.
Now turn to Part Three.

PART 3   *You will hear five different women talking about the activities they enjoy.*
For questions 19 to 23, choose from the list A to F what each speaker says
about her activity. Use the letters only once. There is one extra letter which
you do not need to use.

You now have thirty seconds in which to look at Part Three.

[pause]

tone

Speaker 1:   Well, I suppose I really took up yoga when I left school because there – at school, I mean – they made us take part in all these team games and well, you know it was all about who won and who was best. That's not really me. I was looking for something more . . . um . . . well, more individual really, where I could work within my own limits and not be obliged to compete all the time. So, I can just shut myself away in my room and get on with it.

Speaker 2:   Yes, what I really like about cycling is getting out into the countryside at the weekends and just riding along in the fresh air. I sometimes go for miles, not really thinking about anything. I find it quite restful in a way, you know, just getting away from the stress of living and working in a big city. We often go as a family – me, my husband and the three children – I think it's a good family activity. And then, well, by Monday morning I'm all refreshed and ready for work again.

Speaker 3:   Well, I usually go swimming two or three evenings a week, you know, after work, sometimes I go with colleagues and sometimes on my own. It keeps me fit, you know, and reasonably slim. I learnt when I was about five and I loved it, and I've always kept it up. I think it's something that everybody should learn, whether you want to win races or just get a bit of exercise.

Speaker 4:   Mountaineering always attracted me, even as a child, maybe because where we lived was really flat. I've always dreamed of climbing Mount Everest one day – I suppose all climbers see that as the ultimate challenge. The highest I've been so far since I started climbing at the university was last year when I went to South America. It was fantastic. The great thing is everyone has a part to play. Everyone has to rely on everyone else and you all work together to get to the top.

Speaker 5:   I only started skiing about three years ago, so I'm not very good yet. I love getting up into the mountains, especially early in the morning before there are too many people about and the snow's still fresh. Later in the day's fun too but in a different way, but that first ski of the day is always special. Of course, one of the great things about skiing is there's always plenty to do in the evenings and it's very easy to make friends. I enjoy the company. I just wish I could afford to go more often!

[pause]

tone

Now you'll hear Part Three again.

[The recording is repeated.]

[pause]

That's the end of Part Three.
Now turn to Part Four.

PART 4   *You'll hear a conversation in which Alan asks his friends Bob and Carol about a sports club. Answer questions 24 to 30 by writing B for Bob, C for Carol, or N for Neither in the boxes provided.*

You now have thirty seconds in which to look at Part Four.

[pause]

tone

Alan:	That sports club you both belong to, what's it like Bob?
Bob:	Not bad actually.
Alan:	What can you do there?
Bob:	Oh, the usual things, squash, tennis, swimming pool, fitness classes, all that.
Carol:	But then there are the things you don't find everywhere, like indoor golf and yoga ...
Bob:	Yeah, but Carol you don't ...
Carol:	Yeah, there's not a lot of variety in what I do. I mean, I keep meaning to take up some of the other things, but basically I just use the swimming pool.
Alan:	Doesn't sound bad from what you're saying.
Bob:	Yeah, but I must say some of the equipment has seen better days. I was in the gym the other day using the weights and ... well ... a fair amount of the stuff in there isn't exactly the most up to date.
Carol:	I wouldn't know about that ... I never use it. But you can't really expect perfection for what we pay.
Alan:	I meant to ask you about that, because I'm thinking of joining.
Bob:	Well, they've just put the membership fees up. I don't mind paying a bit more, though ... it's still quite reasonable, considering what you get.
Carol:	Yeah, these places can be quite expensive from what I've seen advertised. This has gone up a bit ... it could be a lot worse, though. I could find out for you how much it is for new members now.
Alan:	What kind of people go there?
Bob:	All sorts. I've met all kinds of people I wouldn't normally run into. There are people of all ages and incomes but everyone gets on well. It doesn't really matter how well off you are when you're running round a tennis court, does it? It can be rather competitive but we also have a laugh a lot of the time.
Carol:	I'm sure I could make friends if I put a bit more effort in. But there isn't a lot of talking in the swimming pool – most people stay on their own or with their own friends. There isn't a lot of mixing in my experience.
Alan:	Actually, I was thinking of taking up some serious fitness training – what are the instructors like?
Bob:	I did a bit of that but I gave it up. It was too much like hard work. The instructors never lost patience with me. Though to be honest I wouldn't blame them if they had. You're supposed to be keen if you take those classes and I was a bit lazy.
Carol:	I did some aqua classes once – that's various kinds of exercises in the water – but I gave it up. They weren't bad, but I got the feeling that the instructors were just there

for the money. They didn't take much interest in us. You didn't get any individual attention, which is what I wanted.

Alan: Well, how about the changing rooms and things like that?

Bob: I've never found the changing rooms I use anything other than spotless, I must say. And the showers, well, I've seen better. But they'll do.

Carol: The changing room I use – the one for the swimming pool – can be pretty mucky. People mention it and they do something about it for a while. But it doesn't last. As for the showers, well, all I'll say is I get in and out as fast as I can.

Alan: Well, maybe I'll join – I probably wouldn't use the pool much anyway.

Bob: We could take you as a guest – guests are free for up to three visits.

Alan: Oh.

Carol: Yeah, why don't you come on Tuesday and see for yourself? We could go for a drink in the Sports Bar Café afterwards.

Alan: Thanks.

Bob: Yeah, that's just opened. It's really convenient to be able to go and have something to eat and drink when you've finished. I thought they were building a bigger place, though. It gets pretty crowded and it can take ages to get served.

Carol: Yeah, but come on! Before that there wasn't anything except a couple of drinks machines. It was really awful. The place really needed something like the new café.

Alan: OK, I'll come on Tuesday.

[pause]

tone

Now you'll hear Part Four again.

[The recording is repeated.]

[pause]

That's the end of Part Four.
There'll now be a pause of five minutes for you to copy your answers onto the separate answer sheet. I'll remind you when there is one minute left, so that you're sure to finish in time.

[pause]

You have one more minute left.

[pause]

That's the end of the test. Please stop now. Your supervisor will now collect all the question papers and answer sheets.
Goodbye.

Test 4 Key

Paper 1 Reading (1 hour 15 minutes)

Part 1
1 F   2 A   3 E   4 G   5 H   6 C   7 B

Part 2
8 B   9 A   10 D   11 A   12 C   13 B   14 A   15 D

Part 3
16 C   17 A   18 F   19 D   20 B   21 E

Part 4
22 B   23 C   24 A   25 B   26 C   27 D   28 C   29 D
30 C   31 A   32 B   33 C   34 D   35 D

Paper 2 Writing (1 hour 30 minutes)

Task-specific mark schemes

Question 1
Content
Major points: All 6 points to be covered. Give brief details of requirements: room for 30 people, date, time. Ask about: meal, drinks and disco.
Minor points: Possible request for vegetarian meal. Any additional information.

Organisation and cohesion
Early reference to why the person is writing. Grouping of ideas into sections giving information and requesting information. Suitable opening and closing formulae.
Not just a list of questions, *unless* the list is introduced appropriately.

Appropriacy of register and format
Letter format. Consistently neutral or formal.

Range
Language appropriate for giving and seeking factual information, and making requests. Present and future forms. Vocabulary to do with arranging a party. Lifting of key words permissible e.g. *disco, meal*.

Target reader
Would be aware of the writer's requirements and be able to respond to questions.

Question 2

Content
Description of *one* special day of a holiday abroad, and an explanation of why it was so exciting (special).

Range
Descriptive and narrative language. Language of explanation. Past tenses.

Organisation and cohesion
Though an article, as a piece of narrative writing it could be minimally paragraphed. There should be a clear link between narration, description and explanation.

Appropriacy of register and format
Range of register is allowable, provided consistent.

Target reader
Would understand why the day was exciting (special).

Question 3

Content
Composition could agree or disagree with the proposition, or discuss both sides of the argument. Should give *some* examples from present and/or past to back up opinion.

Range
Language of comparison and description, opinion and justification. Probably past and present tenses.

Organisation and cohesion
Clear presentation and development of ideas, stating writer's point of view. Appropriate linking of ideas.

Appropriacy of register and format
Neutral composition format.

Target reader
Would be able to understand the writer's viewpoint.

Question 4

Content
State benefits to writer's town – at least *one* each for both park and museum. Statement of preference: clear choice. Reason for preference.

Range
Language of description, comparison, preference, opinion and justification. Present and future tenses (perhaps conditionals and modals).

Organisation and cohesion
Report should be clearly organised. Sub-headings an advantage.

Appropriacy of register and format
Neutral or formal, but must be consistent. Formal report layout not essential.

Target reader
Would understand the choice the writer would make and the writer's reasons for it.

Question 5(a)

Content
Composition could agree or disagree with the proposition, or discuss both sides of the argument. Must refer to the ending in the chosen book.

Range
Language of description, opinion and justification. Range of tenses.

Organisation and cohesion
Clear presentation and development of ideas, including a statement of the writer's point of view. Appropriate linking of description and comment.

Appropriacy of register and format
Neutral composition.

Target reader
Would understand the writer's view of the ending.

Question 5(b)

Content
Make recommendation to read the named book, and give more than one reason for this recommendation. Must *clearly* relate to the book chosen.

Range
Language of description, encouragement, persuasion and justification. Range of tenses.

Organisation and cohesion
Informal letter, with suitable opening and closing formulae, and early reference to reason for writing. Clear presentation and development of ideas. Appropriate linking of recommendation and reasons.

Appropriacy of register and format
Informal letter.

Target reader
Would learn something about the book and why the writer is recommending it. Would want to read the book.

Paper 3 Use of English (1 hour 15 minutes)

Part 1

1 B	2 C	3 A	4 D	5 C	6 B	7 D	8 D	9 A
10 C	11 B	12 D	13 A	14 B	15 C			

Part 2

16 that/which   **17** be   **18** the   **19** part/role   **20** without
21 of   **22** all   **23** sure/certain   **24** run/sell   **25** so
26 are/get   **27** lot   **28** with   **29** aside/away   **30** not/never

Part 3

Award one mark for each correct section.
31 would/'d/should (1) 've/have sent (1)
32 too tired (1) to eat (1)
33 to put (1) up with (1)
34 you mind (1) lending me (1)
35 was not/wasn't allowed (1) to stay (1)
36 did it take (1)(you) to (1)
37 haven't/have not (1) been skiing for (1) OR haven't/have not (1) skied for (1)
38 although (s)he (1) isn't/is not able/is unable (1)
39 are (being) bought (1) by teenagers (1)
40 wish I hadn't/had not (1) invited (1)

Part 4

41 it   **42** being   **43** for   **44** ✓   **45** her   **46** at   **47** to
48 ourselves   **49** ✓   **50** that   **51** ✓   **52** of   **53** ✓
54 our   **55** the

Part 5

56 competition   **57** performance   **58** nervous   **59** successful
60 thoroughly   **61** activity   **62** carefully   **63** imprisoned
64 political   **65** explanation

Paper 4   Listening (40 minutes approximately)

Part 1

1 A   **2** B   **3** A   **4** B   **5** A   **6** B   **7** C   **8** C

Part 2

 9 five/5 (years old)
10 Winter Olympics/Winter Olympic Games
11 North America/Canada (in particular)
12 this season/this year/recently   **13** $3\frac{1}{2}$/three and a half months
14 stay (here/there/in Canada)   **15** most important match/game
16 (the) champion(s)
17 (first team) place/place (in the first team) *not* first place
18 (a) holiday (in Finland)

Part 3

19 F   **20** D   **21** C   **22** E   **23** A

Part 4
24 B   25 A   26 C   27 A   28 B   29 A   30 A

Transcript *First Certificate Listening Test. Test Four.*
Hello. I'm going to give you the instructions for this test. I'll introduce each part of the test and give you time to look at the questions. At the start of each piece you'll hear this sound.

tone

You'll hear each piece twice.

Remember, while you're listening, write your answers on the question paper. You'll have time at the end of the test to copy your answers onto the separate answer sheet.

The tape will now be stopped. Please ask any questions now, because you must not speak during the test.

[pause]

PART 1   *Now open your question paper and look at Part One.*

[pause]

You will hear people talking in eight different situations. For questions 1 to 8, choose the best answer, A, B or C.

Question 1   *One*
Listen to these people talking about an event. What event are they talking about?
A a concert
B a play
C a film

[pause]

tone

Man:	Great, wasn't it!
Woman:	Well, it was OK. I thought the sound could have been a lot better.
Man:	Yeah – but it was just great being there – the atmosphere was incredible.
Woman:	Well, I thought it was too crowded and the guy next to me kept waving his arms about. He really got on my nerves.
Man:	Well, I thought it was brilliant. If they're playing again next month, I'll definitely go again.

[pause]

tone

[The recording is repeated.]

[pause]

Question 2   Two
You hear someone talking about a party he has been invited to. How does he
feel about the party?
A He is nervous about it.
B He thinks it will be boring.
C He is unsure what to expect.

[pause]

tone

Male:	I must admit that I'm not really looking forward to it . . .
Female:	No?
Male:	Well, I've been to their parties before and I don't suppose this one'll be any better . . . all the same people going on and on about their jobs.
Female:	Uh huh
Male:	– they all think they're so important . . . honestly, I just can't face them, I never know what to say! Still I've been invited so I suppose I'd better go.
Female:	Mmm

[pause]

tone

[The recording is repeated.]

[pause]

Question 3   Three
You hear this radio announcement about driving conditions. What is the
main danger tonight?
A ice
B snow
C floods

[pause]

tone

Announcer: With the bad weather continuing, problems are also continuing on the roads. Although river levels have started to fall and further flooding is now unlikely, we are faced tonight with falling temperatures which, combined with wet roads from the earlier flooding, will lead to ice on the roads. The colder weather does mean, however, that there will be little in the way of rain or snow tonight, apart from the odd shower here and there.

[pause]

tone

[The recording is repeated.]

[pause]

Question 4   *Four*
You hear part of a radio play. Where is the scene taking place?
A on a beach
B in a hotel
C in a restaurant

[pause]

tone

Man:	I don't feel too good. I think I might have overdone the sunbathing today.
Woman:	I did warn you – you're not used to all this heat. So, what about dinner?
Man:	I couldn't face anything just now. I think I'll stay in and lie down for a while.
Woman:	You'll probably feel better in a bit. Shall I meet you down here, by the lift, later on then? Maybe we could go to that little place just down the street.
Man:	OK, if I'm feeling better.

[pause]

tone

[The recording is repeated.]

[pause]

Question 5   *Five*
Listen to this woman telling a friend about a television series. What is her opinion of it?
A It is highly original.
B It is very well-acted.
C It is the best series on TV.

[pause]

tone

Woman:	I didn't know what to make of it at first but I really like it now. To be honest some of the acting is a bit, well, unconvincing ... but that's not the point. The stories are so clever ... completely unlike any of that usual detective stuff. You know, in other series the detective always solves the crime. But in this one ... sometimes that doesn't happen. It's one of the programmes I try not to miss.

[pause]

tone

[The recording is repeated.]

[pause]

Question 6   *Six*
You hear someone talking about a hotel. Who is the speaker?
A a hotel receptionist
B a hotel manager
C a hotel chef

[pause]

tone

Man: When I started there, well ... it had been run really badly. The kitchens ... oh dear ... shocking, the waiters and waitresses they were so awful to guests ... constant complaints about the food. The administration ... it was terrible – when guests came to reception they were lucky if anyone could be bothered to deal with them at all. Well, it's all different now – I got rid of a few people ... organised staff training ... anyone can see the whole place is much more efficient now.

[pause]

tone

[The recording is repeated.]

[pause]

Question 7 *Seven*
You hear a British actress, Melina Morton, talking on the radio. Why does Melina live in the USA?
A Her friends are there.
B It's good for her job.
C To be with her husband.

[pause]

tone

Actress: I spend most of my time in the USA these days, we have a house in Connecticut. But, I do get homesick, I love to come home and, luckily, in my job, I seem to be able to once or twice a year because I miss my friends, you know, I miss walking around London and it's ... well, you know if you're born in a place, you always want to come back, at least I know I do. But, since my husband, Mike, has a theatre school, he's a drama and singing coach, and, of course, it was much easier for me to get on a plane and go somewhere to work, than to ask Mike to, you know, suddenly close down the thriving school and try to open one here, you know, it was just not on to do that.

[pause]

tone

[The recording is repeated.]

[pause]

Question 8 *Eight*
You hear someone talking in a tourist information centre. What is the situation?
A She has just arrived in the town.
B She can't find her hotel.
C She has no place to stay.

[pause]

151

tone

Woman: ... so I told them that I wanted the room for another few days but it wasn't possible. I should have told them before, I left it until too late. Anyway, I packed my things and today I've been all over the place, up and down the streets for hours and hours, asking everywhere but I haven't had any success. There aren't any others in my guidebook. So is there anywhere else I can try? I've really enjoyed my time here so far, and I don't want to leave if I can avoid it. Can you help me?

[pause]

tone

[The recording is repeated.]

[pause]

That is the end of Part One.
Now turn to Part Two.

PART 2   *You will hear part of a radio interview with Mikko Korhonen, a Finnish ice hockey star. For questions 9 to 18, complete the sentences which summarise what the ice hockey star says.*

You now have forty-five seconds in which to look at Part Two.

[pause]

tone

Interviewer: Mikko Korhonen is the latest European ice hockey star to cross the Atlantic and join a major team in North America. He left his native Finland to live here in Quebec, in Canada, where he now plays in the National Hockey League. So, Mikko, why did you come all the way to Canada?

Mikko: Well, playing in the National League – the NHL – was a dream I'd had since I was ... I don't know ... since I saw my first game ... I must've been, what, five, I suppose. The only thing that came close to being able to play in the National League was getting the bronze medal for Finland in the Winter Olympics.

The sport in Europe is getting better – the facilities in some places are excellent now and more people are taking an interest – but North America, and Canada in particular, is where it's happening. That's why so many Scandinavians and Russians come here to play. Mind you it took me ages to break into the first team – I didn't manage it until this season. The first game for my Quebec team was incredible. I've been here for four years and I'd given myself until this season to get a first team place. If I hadn't, I'd have given up and gone back to Finland.

Interviewer: But it nearly didn't happen?

Mikko: No, no, that's right. The NHL got involved in an argument with the players and the television companies over money and the team manager stopped all games at national level for three and a half months. You can imagine how I felt! I'd finally been offered the chance to play in a big team and then, just at the start of the season, everything stopped. They were the most depressing months of my life. A lot of players went over to Europe to play, but I thought it would be better for me to stay here.

Interviewer: And now, finally, your dream's come true.

Mikko:	Yeah. For the last four weeks I've been playing here in Quebec and we've hardly lost a game. We've got our most important match early in April. The other team have always been stronger in the past, but this year things are different. We could actually be the champions for the first time in ten years. I can't wait – it'll be a great game! Imagine being in a cup-winning side in my first real season! Everybody seems to be scoring at the moment and my main worry now is keeping my first team place. I haven't got long to prove my worth. My contract's only for one year to begin with, so I'll have to work pretty hard. How I do now will decide my whole future. If everything goes OK, well, I've got a girlfriend here, so I guess if it all works out, I'd like to make my home here permanently. Who knows? – may be one day my children will play for Canada in the Olympics! Mind you, whatever happens this season, I'm planning a holiday in Finland at the end of it.
Interviewer:	Well, thank you, Mikko, and best of luck for the rest of the season!
Mikko:	Thank you.
Interviewer:	And now we move on to rugby . . .

[pause]

tone

Now you'll hear Part Two again.

[The recording is repeated.]

[pause]

That's the end of Part Two.
Now turn to Part Three.

PART 3   *You will hear five people talking about their jobs. For questions 19 to 23, choose which of the opinions A to F each speaker expresses. Use the letters only once. There is one extra letter which you do not need to use.*

You now have thirty seconds in which to look at Part Three.

[pause]

tone

Speaker 1:	Well, being a hotel receptionist suits me down to the ground . . . I mean, I never dreamt I'd end up doing so little but getting a decent salary! I thought when I started that it was going to be a struggle to keep up with everything but it's turned out to be absolutely ideal. There's nothing I can't deal with and some days I'm even looking for things to do! I'm not sure if it's always going to be like that but right now I just can't believe my luck!
Speaker 2:	I might not be making much at the moment but I reckon I will be before too long. You know, the other day, the boss came up to me and said, "Carry on like this and you'll really go places here. You've got a real gift for selling on the phone." Well, I was pretty busy at the time and I didn't take it in till I got home and then I thought, "Nobody in that place has ever said anything like that to me before. I could be on my way up!"
Speaker 3:	What's really different about *this* computing job for me is that, for once, I don't have anyone breathing down my neck all the time. I just get on with my own thing in my own room without anyone bothering me. I've got a lot of responsibility actually, and I

have to watch what decisions I make, but at least I don't have people criticising me all day. Of course, I don't get involved in the office gossip, but well, I don't really miss all that.

Speaker 4: I know this might sound daft, because the job itself is actually rather dull, but I can't wait to go in there in the morning. It doesn't take me long to get there and the journey back's just as quick, but what I really like is how much fun the others are. I know it's not what I'd planned to do, working in a fast food restaurant, and I might not end up doing it for long, but we have such a laugh that it makes up for how boring the work is.

Speaker 5: What appeals to me is that I never know what's going to come up from one day to the next. Sometimes there's not that much on and I can get away early, and other times it's frantic and I have to stay on late. It's certainly good experience if I want to go to a bigger travel agency one day, but I've no plans to at the moment. I mean, there's always something new to learn, something unexpected to deal with.

[pause]

tone

Now you'll hear Part Three again.

[The recording is repeated.]

[pause]

That's the end of Part Three.
Now turn to Part Four.

PART 4   *You will hear an interview about adventure sports. For questions 24 to 30, choose the best answer A, B or C.*

You now have one minute in which to look at Part Four.

[pause]

tone

Interviewer: … Welcome back to the programme. Well, statistics show that the fastest growing sports in Britain are adventure sports and I have with me Stan Leach, an official at the Sports Council, who's going to tell us a bit about some of them. Stan, where shall we start?

Stan: Well, most people start with walking, I think – although of course strictly speaking it's not necessarily an adventure sport, but it's what gets most people outdoors. Indeed, the great thing about walking in Britain is the endless variety, from an easy stroll to a country pub to an energetic walk up a high peak. If you want to take up walking, you can start with a few short circular walks and then pick something longer and more demanding.

Interviewer: What's this thing called scrambling I've been hearing about?

Stan: Yeah, scrambling is sort of in the grey area between walking and climbing. Scrambles are graded according to difficulty, and on the harder ones, which are quite close to rock climbing, it's best to go with an expert.

Interviewer: Well, that brings us nicely on to climbing – that's really caught on here lately, hasn't it?

Stan: Yes, and of course you know it doesn't have to mean going up the really big ones like Everest. Climbing might seem rather terrifying to begin with, but it's great fun and really keeps you fit. You start by climbing small crags before moving on to a rock face. I went for a day's lesson with mountaineer Alan Kimber in Scotland and it was really scary but really exciting.

Interviewer: Right, well, what's next?

Stan: Mountain biking. If you can get used to the saddle, you can cycle across Britain, but unlike in the USA, where there are special cycling paths, in Britain most of the paths are the same as for walkers, which can cause a bit of trouble. After the initial investment – there's one bike that costs £4,000 but you can get a very good one for £200 – it's a cost efficient sport. And there are relatively easy trips such as the Pyrenees Traverse which has 70% downhill slopes with no major climbs.

Interviewer Scuba diving's my personal favourite – any advice on that?

Stan: Yes, swimming underwater opens up a whole new world. Actually, for most people, the idea of being underwater, unable to breathe normally, is a frightening one, but with good tuition you can pick it up in no time at all. Once you get the qualification you need to be considered a competent diver, you can do it anywhere.

Interviewer: I see you've got skydiving on your list. Surely that's only for people who are very brave or mad?

Stan: Well, it is the sort of thing you'd expect to only see in the movies but you'd be amazed how many people go in for it these days. Six hours of training will give you enough background to make the first jump. People who really take to it often join display teams, so if you take it up you might find yourself taking part in special events.

Interviewer: OK, and finally canoeing. That always looks a bit dangerous to me – in that tiny boat with water rushing everywhere.

Stan: Well, there are some terrible bits of water where the real canoeing experts go but beginners can start in gentler waters and build up. There's one stretch in Wales that was designed for the world championships that has a dam release, so that at pre-set times the water runs through. You can phone up and they'll say it's a full release tomorrow or a quarter release, so you can choose your times according to difficulty.

Interviewer: OK, Stan, thanks a lot. After the break, we'll be going to Canada to look at …

[pause]

tone

Now you'll hear Part Four again.

[The recording is repeated.]

[pause]

That's the end of Part Four.
There'll now be a pause of five minutes for you to copy your answers onto the separate answer sheet. I'll remind you when there is one minute left, so that you're sure to finish in time.

[pause]

You have one more minute left.

[pause]

That's the end of the test. Please stop now. Your supervisor will now collect all the question papers and answer sheets.
Goodbye.

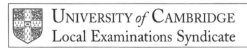

UNIVERSITY *of* CAMBRIDGE
Local Examinations Syndicate

SAMPLE

Candidate Name
If not already printed, write name in CAPITALS and complete the Candidate No. grid (in pencil).

Candidate's signature

- -

Examination Title

Centre

Centre No.

Candidate No.

Examination Details

Supervisor, please complete the details immediately below (in pencil) as applicable.

X   If the candidate is ABSENT or has WITHDRAWN shade here

If a TRANSFERRED CANDIDATE, shade here   and write the original Centre Number here

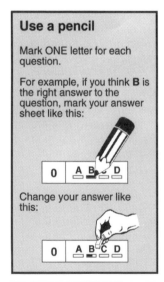

Use a pencil

Mark ONE letter for each question.

For example, if you think **B** is the right answer to the question, mark your answer sheet like this:

0   A B C D

Change your answer like this:

0   A B C D

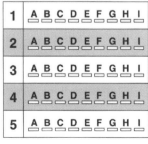

1	A B C D E F G H I
2	A B C D E F G H I
3	A B C D E F G H I
4	A B C D E F G H I
5	A B C D E F G H I

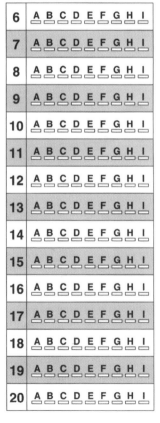

6	A B C D E F G H I
7	A B C D E F G H I
8	A B C D E F G H I
9	A B C D E F G H I
10	A B C D E F G H I
11	A B C D E F G H I
12	A B C D E F G H I
13	A B C D E F G H I
14	A B C D E F G H I
15	A B C D E F G H I
16	A B C D E F G H I
17	A B C D E F G H I
18	A B C D E F G H I
19	A B C D E F G H I
20	A B C D E F G H I

21	A B C D E F G H I
22	A B C D E F G H I
23	A B C D E F G H I
24	A B C D E F G H I
25	A B C D E F G H I
26	A B C D E F G H I
27	A B C D E F G H I
28	A B C D E F G H I
29	A B C D E F G H I
30	A B C D E F G H I
31	A B C D E F G H I
32	A B C D E F G H I
33	A B C D E F G H I
34	A B C D E F G H I
35	A B C D E F G H I

UNIVERSITY *of* CAMBRIDGE
Local Examinations Syndicate

SAMPLE

Candidate Name
If not already printed, write name
in CAPITALS and complete the
Candidate No. grid (in pencil).

Candidate's signature

Examination Title

Centre

Supervisor, please complete the details immediately below (in pencil) as applicable.

[X] If the candidate is ABSENT or has WITHDRAWN shade here ⬜

If a TRANSFERRED CANDIDATE, shade here ⬜ and write the original Centre Number here

Centre No.

Candidate No.

Examination Details

0	0	0	0
1	1	1	1
2	2	2	2
3	3	3	3
4	4	4	4
5	5	5	5
6	6	6	6
7	7	7	7
8	8	8	8
9	9	9	9

Candidate Answer Sheet: FCE paper 3 Use of English

Use a pencil

For **Part 1**: Mark ONE letter for each question.

For example, if you think **C** is the right answer to the question, mark your answer sheet like this:

For **Parts 2, 3, 4** and **5**: Write your answers in the spaces next to the numbers like this:

| 0 | A B C D |

| 0 | *example* |

Part 1				
1	A	B	C	D
2	A	B	C	D
3	A	B	C	D
4	A	B	C	D
5	A	B	C	D
6	A	B	C	D
7	A	B	C	D
8	A	B	C	D
9	A	B	C	D
10	A	B	C	D
11	A	B	C	D
12	A	B	C	D
13	A	B	C	D
14	A	B	C	D
15	A	B	C	D

Part 2	Do not write here
16	16
17	17
18	18
19	19
20	20
21	21
22	22
23	23
24	24
25	25
26	26
27	27
28	28
29	29
30	30

Turn over for Parts 3 - 5 →

157

SAMPLE

Part 3		Do not write here
31		31 0 1 2
32		32 0 1 2
33		33 0 1 2
34		34 0 1 2
35		35 0 1 2
36		96 0 1 2
37		37 0 1 2
38		38 0 1 2
39		39 0 1 2
40		40 0 1 2

Part 4		Do not write here
41		41
42		42
43		43
44		44
45		45
46		46
47		47
48		48
49		49
50		50
51		51
52		52
53		53
54		54
55		55

Part 5		Do not write here
56		56
57		57
58		58
59		59
60		60
61		61
62		62
63		63
64		64
65		65

SAMPLE

Candidate Name
If not already printed, write name
in CAPITALS and complete the
Candidate No. grid (in pencil).

Candidate's signature

Examination Title

Centre

Centre No.

Candidate No.

Examination Details

Supervisor, please complete the details immediately below (in pencil) as applicable.

☒ If the candidate is ABSENT or has WITHDRAWN shade here ▭

If a TRANSFERRED CANDIDATE, shade here ▭ and write the original Centre Number here

Candidate Answer Sheet: FCE paper 4 Listening

Mark test version below

A	B	C	D	E

Special arrangements S   H

Use a pencil

For **Parts 1** and **3**:
Mark ONE letter for
each question.

For example, if you
think **B** is the right
answer to the
question, mark your
answer sheet like this:

0	A	B	C

For **Parts 2** and **4**:
Write your answers in
the spaces next to the
numbers like this:

0	*example*

Part 1

1	A	B	C
2	A	B	C
3	A	B	C
4	A	B	C
5	A	B	C
6	A	B	C
7	A	B	C
8	A	B	C

Part 2

	Do not write here
9	9
10	10
11	11
12	12
13	13
14	14
15	15
16	16
17	17
18	18

Part 3

19	A	B	C	D	E	F
20	A	B	C	D	E	F
21	A	B	C	D	E	F
22	A	B	C	D	E	F
23	A	B	C	D	E	F

Part 4

	Do not write here
24	24
25	25
26	26
27	27
28	28
29	29
30	30

159